MW01070178

Back To
BASICS

Dog Training By
FABIAN

Back To
BASICS

Dog Training By
FABIAN

Written By
ANDREA ARDEN

With photos by
GREGOR HALENDA and CHRIS RAMIREZ

Howell Book House
New York

HOWELL BOOK HOUSE
A Simon & Schuster Macmillan Company
1633 Broadway
New York, NY 10019

Copyright © 1997 by Fabian Robinson and Andrea Arden

All rights reserved. No part of this book shall be reproduced, stored in a retrieval system, or transmitted by any means, electronic, mechanical, photocopying, recording, or otherwise without written permission from the publisher. No patent liability is assumed with respect to the use of the information contained herein. Although every precaution has been taken in preparation of this book, the publisher and authors assume no responsibility for errors or omissions. Neither is any liability assumed for damages resulting from the use of the information contained herein. For information, address Howell Book House, 1633 Broadway, 7th Floor, New York, NY 10019-6785.

MACMILLAN is a registered trademark of Macmillan, Inc.

Library of Congress Cataloging-in Publication Data

Arden, Andrea and Fabian Robinson
    Back to basics : dog training by Fabian / written by
Andrea Arden ; with photos by Gregor Halenda and Chris
Ramirez.
        p.   cm.
    ISBN 0-87605-582-X
    1. Dogs—Training.   I. Robinson, Fabian.   II. Title.
SF431.A74   1997
636.7'0887—dc21   97-12285
                                         CIP

Manufactured in the United States of America

99 98 97   9 8 7 6 5 4 3 2

Text and Cover Design by designLab, Seattle

TABLE OF CONTENTS

ACKNOWLEDGMENTS

We would like to thank all of the people and their dogs who generously gave of their time to be a part of this book: Nathan Barotz and Sherlock, Rhett Butler and Lena, Michelle Coniker and Jada, Kate Daisley and Herbie, Laura Falter, the Guttstein family and Rusty, Greg Kahn and Kash, Lauren Klejmont and Eko, Jill Lawrence and Max, Brian Michalski, Tim and Sarah Miller and Buddy, Elizabeth and Mathew Oldroyd and Uri, John Roberts, John Shegda and Madison, Doris Stohl and Nathan and Shmooey, Jane Timken and Finn, Amelia and Stephen Verlin and Molly and Freckles, and Todd Yoggy and Albert.

Enormous thanks to Gregor Halenda and Chris Ramirez, who took the photos in this book and made us all look good.

Personal acknowledgments from Fabian: Many thanks go to my wife, Sharlene, for her constant support and to my daughters, Rachel and Ciara, and of course to Striker.

Personal acknowledgments from Andrea: Thanks to my brother George, who helped me to learn the importance of strength and looking at the bright side, and to Oliver, the dog who changed my life.

WHY IS THIS TRAINING BOOK DIFFERENT?

This book explains the method of training dogs developed by Fabian Robinson, and is the result of a collaboration between Fabian and Andrea Arden. Fabian explained how frustrated he felt about the current state of pet dog training. Both Fabian and Andrea believe that too many dogs suffer as a result of the confusing and often inaccurate information that is provided to pet owners.

This book looks to facilitate training by using rapid and effective techniques. Dog training should be fast and simple—otherwise it is of little benefit to dog or owner. A drawn-out training regimen is a frustrating and tiresome process which the owner usually won't stick with for long. It's also not the ideal way for a dog to learn. Keep in mind how quickly a dog in the wild must learn in order to survive: A wild dog who investigates a porcupine will learn very quickly why it shouldn't. For dogs in the wild, their survival depends on learning the dos and don'ts very fast. The same holds true in your home.

The basic training concepts in this book are easy to understand and apply. There are only four commands

Using the basic commands in real life will determine how your dog behaves. This dog sits politely at the corner before crossing.

that need to be taught and just a few concepts that owners must understand and embrace. We have broken the training down into four basic steps. The first is the concept of creating a fracture. If you have owned your dog for more than one month, it is most likely that you and your dog have both developed habits that do not lend themselves to a positive dog–human relationship. You may be verbally reprimanding your dog, which breaks down communication and trust, and your dog may be quickly developing behaviors, such as house soiling, that you will be unwilling to live with for very long. In this case, you and your dog need the opportunity to start fresh; creating a fracture does just this.

Once you have wiped the slate clean for learning, your dog is ready to be taught the four basic commands—Sit, Down, Come and Release. The process of teaching these commands is called foundation training. This should take no more than a few days for the average dog.

Once you are sure your dog understands the meaning of each command, it is unnecessary to continue to set aside training sessions throughout the day. Instead, you will immediately use the commands for the purposes they were intended: real life situations. This is called lifestyle training.

How you use the commands in real life depends on how you expect your dog to behave. For example, if you want him to greet people politely, you will make him sit to greet people. If you don't want him to beg for food at the table, you can make him lie down a few feet away from you while you eat. Soon your dog will automatically sit when someone comes up to say hello and will lie down when your family sits down to eat. He has learned what behaviors are appropriate and he behaves accordingly out of habit.

Finally, this book will explain how to properly administer a correction to your dog. Corrections are never intended to frighten or harm a dog, only to teach. Still, corrections are negative experiences, and that's why they should never come from you. There are ways to make your dog think corrections stem directly from incorrect behavior, while you provide only praise.

Just about anyone is capable of training their dog. The ingredients are simple: the right information, and confidence. Don't be too concerned if you don't consider yourself a very patient person—it isn't really a key ingredient to training, especially when the training is so quick. Imagine you are going on a trip and someone has given you very clear instructions on how to get where you are going. In this case, you don't really need much patience, just a bit of time and the confidence to follow the instructions. The same holds true when teaching your dog.

Many people who come to us have been to see other trainers before. In a lot of these cases we are asked to critique the other trainer's methods. We are understandably wary to do so. However, it is important for people to understand why certain "modern"

There's no magic to successful dog training. All you need are confidence and the right information.

methods are not successful. When you attempt to train your dog following the method of this or that expert, it's tempting to blame the dog if you're unsuccessful. That's how many dogs get labeled stubborn or stupid.

In fact, not all training theories are correct. It is important to explain the inaccuracies in some training theories so that you may clearly understand why they should probably be avoided. For example, it is often suggested to owners that their tone of voice is a key ingredient in training. This is completely untrue. Commands should not be given in any specific tone, and corrections should not be verbal. You should be able to speak to your dog in your normal voice; who wants to have to speak firmly to their dog in order to have him comply? Furthermore, if your dog is taught to obey the tone of your voice rather than the words you say, you will always have to say a command in a certain tone. We want to teach our dogs the *meaning* of words, not tones of voice. If the dog is taught to understand the meaning of a word, you should be able to whisper a command and he should obey.

You should also try to avoid using your voice to correct your dog. It is unpleasant to have to verbally reprimand your dog, but more important, it is detrimental to the training process. By associating yourself with a negative, you are making yourself part of the problem in your dog's eyes. We want dogs to understand that their actions alone are what cause negatives, not us. So, as much as possible we like to encourage owners to associate themselves only with praise and guidance.

A person who constantly yells at her dog for snooping in the garbage will teach the dog not to do so when people are home. But, when he is on his own and nobody is there to yell at him, why shouldn't he check out the garbage? In order for the dog to decide for himself that he doesn't want to snoop in the garbage, whether someone is home or not, there must be a negative consequence for doing so that occurs regardless of who else is in the home at the time. If you always step in to make choices for your dog, you will have a dog who always requires you to be there in order to make the right choices.

Negative consequences, then, are not something administered by the trainer (that's you), but rather occur as a result of something the dog has done. Consequently, the dog thinks about what has happened and decides he would rather avoid the unpleasant experience. His trainer is always the source of *positive* reinforcement.

Dogs should be allowed to use their natural reasoning powers to learn. They can figure out that certain behaviors result in positive outcomes and others in negative. If you shout at your dog when he behaves inappropriately, he will obviously be more focused on you than on figuring out the relationship between his behavior and the outcome.

An example of allowing the negative to result solely from the dog's actions would be to set up a booby trap. Tying a few throw cans together, attaching the rope to the garbage bin, and then placing them on a counter above the bin is just such a trap: The throw cans will crash down on the dog when he tips the garbage over. Throw cans don't hurt the dog—there are just a few pennies in each otherwise empty can—but they certainly do startle him. This experience, especially if repeated two to three times, will make the dog think searching in the garbage is not so much fun after all.

There is a strong movement toward using strictly positive reinforcement to train dogs. The idea that this is an effective method is another falsehood that does an enormous disservice to dogs. In reality, no creature can be expected to learn without the balance of positive and negative. There must be consequences for inappropriate behavior. This is why we have laws that set down the criteria for our society's expectations and the consequences for not living up to them. Consequences are meant to teach, not to harm. In reality, the absence of a balance of positive and negative consequences are what will do the most harm to your dog. He will be ill equipped to survive in our world if he doesn't have the capacity to understand why he should behave in certain ways and not in others.

There are no mysteries in dog training. Dogs learn through a process of association. By associating an action with a consequence, which can be either positive or negative, the likelihood of repeating that action is determined. If an action results in a positive consequence, for example if begging at the table gets the dog a few treats, then it will probably occur again as the dog tries to repeat the positive outcome. If an action results in a negative consequence, for example if lunging at the end of a leash results in a leash snap correction, then it will probably not occur again as the dog tries to avoid the negative outcome.

Dogs are well equipped to figure out what will benefit their survival. The best thing we can do to help them is to set out clear problems and encourage them to choose the answer that best benefits their survival in our society.

As training proceeds, the dog becomes more adept at thinking through each learning experience. The average pet owner wants a dog who knows how to

To survive in our world, a dog must know how to behave in all kinds of situations.

behave at home with the family and guests, or out in public surrounded by strangers and countless distractions. In these situations the dog must have the capacity to choose how to behave appropriately. Using this book as a guide, you have the ability to teach your dog to be a thinking member of society.

ABOUT YOU

You are the most important component of your dog's training. You are the one who will show your dog how to behave in order to fit into your world. The most significant thing you can do to make this process easier for both of you is to decide what you want from your dog. Think of yourself as your dog's coach. Before the game begins, a good coach sets out a clear game plan of what he expects from his players. A good dog owner should make a list of what he expects from his dog; think of it as your dog's game plan for life. You'll plan out the game he'll play, teach him how to play it, and routinely judge his performance.

EXPECTATIONS

To begin your effective training program, you will need to write down a list of what you expect from your dog. If you are not perfectly clear in this regard, then it is unfair to expect your dog to know what you want. There are two categories of expectations that domesticated dogs live by: society's expectations and our own.

It is not unreasonable to expect your dog to behave appropriately around other people.

Many people don't mind having a small dog jump on them to say hello.

No matter what type, size, or age of dog you own, society expects it to behave according to a set code of conduct. Basically, this requires that your dog behave appropriately around people and be trained to eliminate in appropriate spots out of doors, or in some cases on paper indoors. Failing to adhere to either one of these two basic rules lands many dogs in a shelter.

While all domesticated dogs must live by the same general rules in order to be accepted, there are more specific rules you need to set down so that your dog will fit into your particular life. This is analogous to there being federal laws that everyone must follow, regardless of which state you live in, and other laws that are unique to each state. Look at each home as a state with its own unique rules.

Imagine how your ideal dog would behave—that is what you will train your dog to do. You have the ability and the responsibility to teach your dog to fit that ideal as closely as possible.

You must be perfectly clear on what your rules are. After all, if you aren't clear, how can you expect your dog to be? This means if someone asks you if your dog is allowed on the furniture, you must be able to answer assertively. What is your dog supposed to do when you are eating dinner? Where is he supposed to sleep? How is he supposed to greet strangers? We suggest writing down these expectations and rules so you and everyone else in the household are perfectly clear on the rules your dog is expected to live by.

This list of behaviors that makes up your ideal dog will become part of your dog's lifestyle only if you stick to it. Pretty soon, enforcing a Down on a blanket while you watch television will become so normal to your dog that when he sees you turning on the television, he will head over to his blanket out of habit. This applies to almost all of the behaviors you teach your dog to follow; after a period of time they

A large dog who jumps to greet people can be a nuisance and a danger.

it is realistic. If you make it a rule that your dog is not allowed on the couch, will all members of your household enforce this rule? If you're not sure, don't make this a rule because the dog will learn that at certain times and with certain people he doesn't have to live the lifestyle you have chosen. This sort of situation only leads to confusion on everyone's part.

Fairness to your dog should also be a consideration as you decide on the rules. Most dogs, if trained properly, can live up to even the highest expectations; guide dogs are a wonderful example of this. However, be fair to your dog. A dog is a dog, after all. They all have the propensity to play, run, chase, bark, dig, and so on. Allow him the freedom to enjoy being a dog, but remember he can do so only within the boundaries you set. He can run and chase when you teach him to retrieve, or bark when you teach him to speak on command. Just as we learn to enjoy life within the confines of civilized society, so can your dog—with help from you.

will become habit, but only if you regularly enforce them.

BE REALISTIC AND FAIR

When deciding on the lifestyle you are going to train your dog to become accustomed to, consider whether

DON'T FEEL SORRY FOR YOUR DOG

If you are realistic and fair, there is no need to feel sorry for your dog. Abiding by rules and boundaries is part of everyone's life. Besides, feeling sorry for dogs (and not setting rules for them) often means they end up in animal shelters labeled as unruly and untrainable. The old saying "killing with kindness" is all too true for many dogs in America.

Consider this scenario: A family brings home their new puppy, and the very first day they let him run all over the living room to play with the neighbor's children, who have come over to see him. He eliminates all over the room and plays wildly with the children, nipping at their hair and clothes. They call a local trainer, who tells them to confine the puppy to a small area and take him outside frequently, where they will praise him for eliminating in the right spot.

The owners think it is mean to keep the puppy "locked up," so they continue to let him be free in the house. When he goes on the rug they yell at him, so the puppy learns that people don't like to see him eliminate. He starts to relieve himself behind the couch where nobody can see him. After a few weeks the family gets tired of cleaning up the pup's mess, so they decide to keep him outside. The puppy ends up spending more and more time by himself; he can't come inside because he isn't house trained. He gets lonely, so he barks and digs. The neighbors complain, and finally the family gives up and takes the adolescent dog to the shelter. They tell the volunteers that he is just too unruly and stubborn.

This dog's life would probably have been much more pleasant if the family had reevaluated what kindness really means. In this dog's case, as in most, it means clearly and humanely showing your dog what it is you expect of him and helping him to achieve it.

THE DOG'S POINT OF VIEW

Think of your dog as a foreign exchange student who doesn't understand the local language or laws. Just as an exchange student would be grateful for a guide who explains the laws and customs of a foreign land, your dog will feel the same way when you create a guide for him. Your list of expectations and rules is the first step in successfully teaching your dog to live in the human world.

ABOUT YOUR DOG

STOP SEEING YOUR DOG AS A PACK ANIMAL

Dog pack structure and behavior is a very interesting subject, but it should not play as strong a role in dog training as it has. This is because it is impossible for us to accurately imitate gestures that require a subtle mixture of canine body language and vocalization.

Human imitations of dog behavior are sure to get both handler and dog into serious trouble. For example, the alpha roll, used to teach a dog to be submissive, is usually described as pinning the dog down on his back until he stops struggling. But more often than not this turns out as follows: The owner pins the dog, who understandably struggles, maybe because he dislikes being in a submissive position but more likely out of an innate fear of being under attack from a predator.

There are then two likely outcomes. The first is that the owner will be able to hold the dog down until it submits. This may give the owner a false sense of control and dominance. Who is to say that this animal will continue to submit to physical force? The day may come when the dog fights back using his teeth and does serious damage.

The second is that the owner, usually a novice, will be ill equipped to deal with the dog's understandable struggle to be released. The owner may release the dog if he starts to squeal, claw, or bite. In this case, the owner may lose faith in his ability to train the dog and the dog has learned, among other things, that he can get out of some situations by squealing, clawing and biting.

Another example of the intricacies of dog behavior is the mother dog who warns her puppy and then corrects. There is exquisite timing involved in both the warning and the correction that most humans could not possibly imitate. While there are some exaggerated and general gestures you can make that are often properly interpreted by your dog, such as the play bow, the vast majority of canine communication is out of the range of the average person's abilities.

Before you brought your puppy or dog home, did you think of your family as a pack of animals? The answer is probably no, in which case the next question is, why would you allow a dog to come into your home and change your way of thinking?

Our dogs are already experts in dog behavior; we can't teach them anything about it that they don't already know. Our job is to teach them about human behavior. This is how we will domesticate our dogs.

Dogs are not born domesticated, even though we refer to them as domesticated animals. If there were a litter of pups in your backyard and you never touched them, spoke to them, or went anywhere near them, they would not grow up to be domesticated dogs. While the mere proximity of humans would make them different from feral dogs, they would be ill equipped to live in your home.

All dogs are born with an innate pack mentality. This means they are born with the instincts to survive as a member of a pack of dogs. We domesticate dogs—make them more adaptable to living in human society—beginning the moment we lay our hands on them as newborns. But full and proper domestication of a dog is a process that takes quite a bit of time and usually continues well into the dog's adolescence.

NATURAL INSTINCTS

Instincts are what enable an animal to survive in the environment it was born to live in. Your dog is born with instincts that will help him to survive in a dog pack, but not necessarily in your home. Some of your dog's instinctual behaviors include digging, barking, chewing, chasing, marking with urine and displaying aggression. These behaviors each have a purpose: Chewing keeps teeth healthy; barking sends a variety of messages and warnings; digging is to bury food for later, to find warmth in the cold weather and cool earth in the hot weather and to protect puppies; chasing and herding are to hunt down prey; urine marking is to establish territory; and displays of aggression help establish pack order and serve as warnings, among other functions.

Instinctual behaviors cannot be changed, but they can be redirected. For example, a dog with a strong instinctual drive to chase can be encouraged to redirect his chasing from something you find inappropriate, such as cats or children, to something more appropriate, like a ball. It would be unfair and unrealistic to expect your dog to stifle all of his instincts, so be sure to offer your dog mental and physical stimulation that will allow him to play out some of his instinctual drives in appropriate ways.

Your dog is not going to live in a dog pack, he is going to live with you. In this environment many of his instinctual behaviors will do him no good. However, some of them will. If focused correctly, these instincts can serve to benefit owners and, in turn, dogs, because they become more positively involved in their human family. For example, a dog's

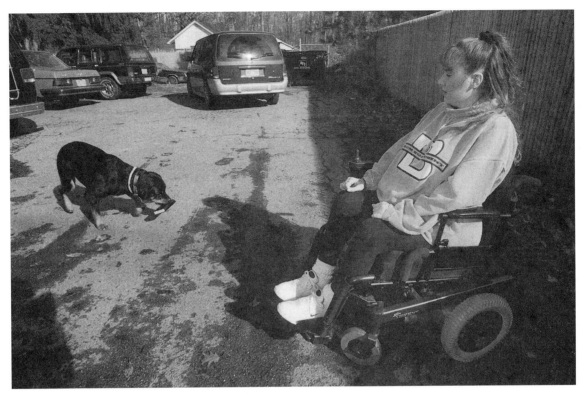

Jada, a Rottweiler, retrieves an object for Michelle.

natural chase instinct can be developed into a retrieve. Many dogs are trained to assist physically challenged people by retrieving objects for them.

On the down side, if we allow certain instincts to develop, they may be detrimental to the dog's survival in human society. For example, people often are delighted when their new puppy exhibits doggy behaviors, such as his first play growl, or when he chases and tackles one of his litter mates. But it is important to remember that the pup is not exhibiting these behaviors for our amusement. Rather, he is instinctively practicing those behaviors that would best help him to survive in a wild dog pack. If left unchecked, the pup will develop behaviors that will make it more difficult for him to survive in our world. A dog who hunts, chases and bites whatever he wants will probably not survive in our world for long.

YOUR DOG'S SENSES

How your dog sees the world makes a big difference in how you train him. Dogs rely on scent and sound much more than we do, for instance, and there are ways you can use that to help your dog learn what he needs to know in order to survive in our world.

Sight Because dogs are predatory animals, most have fairly good eyesight. However, they are more proficient at detecting movement than at seeing specific detailed gestures. Dogs tend to be shortsighted and do not see in the same detailed way that we do. This is part of the reason dogs do not use sight to recognize us, as much as smell and sound.

The positioning of the dog's eyes on his head allows for a wide range of vision, and dogs tend to have better peripheral vision than we do. Obviously, there is a wide variation in the way different breeds look, so eye position does vary. The original purpose of the breed also explains some variations in visual acuity. Some breeds, such as the Whippet, have very good sight at far distances, while others have better sight at close range.

Smell Smell is one of the dog's keenest senses. Dogs can interpret sources of food and danger using their sense of smell. They can tell what other animals have passed through their territory, how long ago, and even the sex of those intruders.

Our own sense of smell is so limited in comparison that it's hard to even imagine what the world smells like to a dog. For example, while we consider

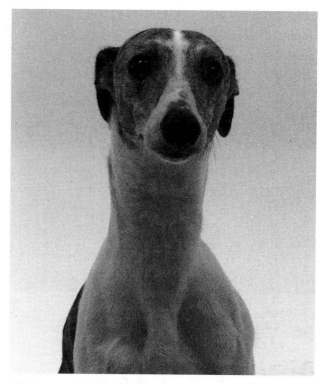

Whippets were originally bred to have very good sight in order to swiftly hone in on fast-moving prey.

salt to be basically odorless, a dog can smell a teaspoonful of salt dissolved in 13 gallons of water.

The dog's sense of smell is so acute that they can sense even very subtle changes in our emotional state. What they are smelling is the release of certain chemicals through the sweat glands of our skin. This may help to explain why your dog looks "guilty" when you arrive home to find he has been destructive in some way. It is likely that in the split second you become aware of his behavior your body is emitting odors that your dog smells.

The dog's incredibly sensitive sense of smell can be a training tool, used to both reward and correct your dog. For example, a collar that emits an unpleasant odor when the dog barks (called the Aboistop collar) can discourage the dog from doing so.

Taste The dog's sense of taste is similar to ours in that he experiences the same four basic taste categories: sweet, sour, salty and bitter. Taste can also be used to aid in training, particularly when you use commercial products, such as Bitter Apple, that have a bad taste. And of course, food is a wonderful bonus reward for many dogs.

Hearing Most dogs have a very keen sense of hearing. This is one of the many reasons why it is unrealistic to believe you must scream a command at an animal who is no more than 10 or 15 feet away from you.

Dogs hear a much wider range of sounds than we do, and just like us, they can "tune out" certain sounds. Using your voice to incessantly correct your dog will probably overstimulate him to the point where he will begin to block out your voice. Instead, use your normal tone of voice to give commands and to offer praise and encouragement to your dog. In this way, you will be making the meaning of your voice clear to your dog. When he hears it, he will pay immediate attention because it always means good things. Talking too much to your dog is one of the hardest habits for owners to break, because humans primarily communicate verbally.

Touch As with people, there is an enormous range in the level of touch sensitivity that individual dogs experience. There is also a vast range in sensitivity depending on the area of the body being touched. Some dogs are extremely sensitive in the flank area or near their ears, while it can be difficult to find touch-sensitive areas on other dogs. Minimal touch sensitivity is a trait that has been selectively bred for in a number of breeds, especially fighting and hunting dogs. However, this does not mean every individual dog of that breed is less sensitive to touch.

Touch can be a very effective tool in training dogs. For example, placing a dog in a sit with a touch can serve as an automatic signal when the area is too crowded or noisy for you to give a verbal command.

DOG LANGUAGE

Dogs use a variety of their senses when they communicate with each other. They emit smells, make sounds and display a range of body postures that would be nearly impossible for humans to accurately imitate. Broad gestures of communication, such as the play bow (when a dog stretches out his front legs, lowering his head and raising his rear in the air), most humans can accurately communicate to dogs. However, to try to imitate the way a mother dog growls at her puppies, or to scruff shake an adult dog (or a puppy, for that matter) can be dangerous and confusing to dogs

These two puppies, a Bulldog and a Jack Russell Terrier, are saying quite a bit to each other through both subtle and obvious body cues and vocalizations.

and owners, because so much is lost in the translation that we often are not really communicating what we think we are.

Mounting is another way dogs communicate. Dogs mount each other to establish dominance and, of course, to reproduce. An adolescent dog who ignores an older dog's growls intended to stop him from mounting is looking to usurp the older dog's dominance. People sometimes think it is cute or funny for a young puppy to mount people's legs or pillows, but this can turn into a serious problem. A dog mounting a person may be testing his dominance over you. The dog should be corrected immediately

for mounting, especially children. (See Chapter Eight for more on dealing with mounting.)

Subtle signs we may not even notice send clear signals to other dogs. If a dog's mouth is closed when he is being approached, for example, this might be an indication that he is not receptive to the approach. This is usually accompanied by a stiffening of the dog's body and a hard glare.

Raised hackles can be another warning sign. A dog's hackles are located on his back, directly behind the base of the neck. When the hair in this region is raised, it is meant to make the dog look larger and more intimidating. This is a dog that doesn't have total confidence and needs some backup.

A relaxed and confident dog will usually carry his tail somewhere between his hocks (the lower part of the back legs) and level with his back. His mouth will usually be at least slightly open and his general body posture will be soft and relaxed.

A dog who is displaying dominance will usually have a stiff posture. The ears will be as erect as possible—even for drop-eared dogs you will notice a slight lift—and the tail will be held as erect as possible. A dominant dog facing down an opponent will usually have his mouth closed.

A shy or less confident dog will usually lower his head and body, with his ears flat back and his tail tucked between his legs. The more frightened and insecure the dog, the smaller they want to become. He will tend to avoid eye contact and back away. The dog may even submissively urinate, especially a younger dog.

Another sign of submissiveness is rolling on the back. Of course, it can also mean the dog is relaxed and simply wants a good tummy rub. A dog that refuses to roll over doesn't want to be in a vulnerable position and is not willing to be submissive. If you have an older puppy or adult dog who shows this behavior, you should work on establishing more control using the four basic obedience commands outlined in this book (Release, Sit, Down and Come).

A wagging tail is probably the dog behavior that is most often misinterpreted by humans. A wagging tail is not necessarily an indication that a dog is feeling friendly. Dogs also wag their tails when they're nervous. If a tail is carried high over a dog's back and is wagging in a short, fast rhythm, the dog may be expressing dominance or conflict. Such a dog should obviously not be approached.

Another behavior that can have several meanings is growling. When two dogs are playing and you hear growling, it's good to know the difference between a friendly growl and an aggressive growl. A friendly growl is when the dogs have a relaxed posture and their tails are wagging. If a dog's tail is raised higher over the back than usual it may be an indication that the dog is displaying dominance.

When a growl is outright aggressive, the dog's posture is stiff and movement becomes slower. He may try to establish dominance by attempting to stand over the other dog, placing a paw on the other dog's back or putting his head over the dog's withers (where the neck meets the back). If the dogs start developing strong, hard eye contact with each other a fight is likely to break out, unless one dog backs down.

DEVELOPING A PEOPLE-CENTERED DOG

To survive in our environment it is necessary to help your dog develop a fondness for spending time with people. This is usually a bit more difficult if you have more than one dog. The majority of your dog's play time should be spent with you, not another dog. Otherwise, you risk losing control of your dog because

This Bulldog puppy may be attempting to show dominance over this adult female German Shepherd by placing his paws on her back.

She quickly makes it clear to him that she finds this unacceptable.

nature will take over and the dogs may be more concerned with their own relationship than with you. Obviously, neither dog is equipped to teach the other how to survive in the human world—only you are.

It is in your dog's best interest to be focused on you. He should see you as a kind of safety net, because in reality that is what you are to him. You are the one who will guide him through the obstacles of a world in which all the rules and methods of communication are very foreign to dogs.

CHARACTER TRAITS

Character, sometimes also called temperament, is genetically based in dogs. Some research suggests that it is due, in part, to such things as the number of puppies in a litter, the ratio of males to females and placement in the womb. For example, a litter with one female and three males might produce a female with a slightly stronger character than a litter of three females and one male. Your dog's basic character is something he is born with—it's a done deal.

All dogs have basically the same capacity for the same feelings and behaviors, such as aggression or fear, but the level to which these surface is what makes up the dog's basic character. Some breeds of dogs have been bred to manifest certain traits more strongly. For example, dogs used for police work are required to be more sensitive to various stimuli so that they will be more alert, but this does not mean police dogs have a monopoly on this characteristic.

Environment cannot change a dog's character, but it can have an enormous impact on the direction the innate character of a dog is allowed to take. Many breeds that have been stereotyped as highly aggressive have been raised in environments where this behavior was fostered. This means that the owner, whether knowingly or unknowingly, allowed the young dog to develop a habit of behaving aggressively. Often in situations like this, when the dog reaches maturity this behavior is blamed on the breed's character. But just as a child who grows up without any discipline is likely to have a troubled future, so is a dog. A child—or a dog—who grows up in a disciplined environment and is taught the skills necessary to survive successfully in society has a great head start, no matter what his basic character is.

WHAT ABOUT BREEDS?

The greatest and most obvious difference between breeds of dogs is the packaging. People have invested an enormous amount of time and energy into developing dogs who come closest to what they consider a physical ideal. A breeder who believes that a perfect specimen of a breed should have an extremely long coat will breed together two dogs who have very long coats and whose ancestors had long coats. But when it comes down to it, a dog is a dog is a dog. A Chihuahua is as much of a dog as a Mastiff or an Airedale.

No one breed or type of dog has a monopoly on any character traits. All dogs have the same underlying

On the outside this Papillon and Tosa Inu could not be more different, but they both possess the same basic character traits found in all canines.

traits; it is the degree to which each trait surfaces that distinguishes one dog's character from another. Breeders can selectively breed to exaggerate or diminish character traits, but within a breed there will be an enormous range of personalities, some of which will personify the breed's stereotype and some of which will totally go against the breed stereotype.

Furthermore, within a litter of dogs you will find a range of characters. Each dog has its own distinctive character.

When choosing a dog it can be helpful to research what the breed was developed to do. This will give you a general idea of what the surface traits of the breed will be. However, not all working dogs have a working dog temperament, not all sporting dogs have a sporting dog temperament, and so on. Even dogs bred to do a specific task must be introduced to that task at a very young age in order to nurture the behavior. So a breed bred to fight would also need to be allowed to develop that behavior. If it's not taught how to behave in our society, any dog of any breed or mix of breeds can become shy or aggressive, or otherwise behave inappropriately. It is more important to evaluate the individual dog you are choosing and that dog's immediate ancestors than the breed as a whole.

The ancestors of your potential new pet will tell you more about your dog than any general breed reference book. If the dog is one of the sporting breeds, has the breeder bred selectively for dogs who are good hunters or for dogs who have good temperament, who are healthy or who look pretty? (If they are truly interested in benefiting the future of the breed, the answer would be all of these.) If you have chosen a working dog, such as a Rottweiler or a Doberman Pinscher, does the dog's background include relatives who were involved in Ring Sport or protection work? The goals of the breeding program of that particular dog will tell you more about his potential character than the breed standard will.

This means if you are interested in owning a dog with strong herding abilities you should consider getting a dog whose dam and sire are proven to have strong herding abilities. However, just because the mother and father have a strong herding drive does not necessarily mean the offspring will. Just as with people, genetic traits are all passed on in different degrees to different offspring. Your parents may be very musically inclined, but this doesn't guarantee that you will be. And if you grow up in an environment with no music at all, your genetic heritage may never manifest itself. The same is true with dogs.

Many people will argue this point and say they are sure some breeds are smarter, quicker, more eager to please or more stubborn than others. Yes, it is fair to say there are some accurate breed generalizations. However, the majority of these generalizations have far more to do with environment and specific breedings than with anything else.

It is fair to say a good percentage of terriers are feisty, but not necessarily because they are terriers. Rather, it's because they tend to be smaller dogs and owners tend to allow smaller dogs to get away with more than bigger dogs. If a small dog pulls on the leash it isn't usually so bad and you might just pick the dog up. The average Airedale is not as feisty as most other terriers because Airedales are bigger and aren't usually allowed to get away with so much.

Sometimes a generalization about a breed becomes a self-fulfilling prophecy. Most people choose certain breeds because of the breeds' stereotypical characteristics. These are characteristics they want and will seek out. So if you want a tough dog and have heard Rottweilers are tough, you'll seek out the toughest Rottweiler you can find and pass up the ones that seem more gentle. Further, you might encourage your dog to act tough.

Many breed stereotypes are perpetuated this way. If you get a little puppy and from the first day you bring it home you call it stubborn, that is most likely how it will turn out. You may inadvertently be allowing this "stubborn streak" to develop. If you get a dog thinking he will be very smart and well behaved, he is more likely to be.

All breeds of dogs have the potential to be wonderful pets with the right guidance and supervision.

No one breed has a lock on aggression, shyness, stubbornness, retrieving ability, herding ability or trainability. Professional trainers all too often hear phrases like: "My terrier is really stubborn, you know how terriers are," "Rottweilers are really mean dogs, aren't they?" "My friend had a setter and she said they're all really hyper." Statements like these serve one purpose: To put blame for inappropriate behaviors on the dog or its breed. A particular breed or pedigree does not guarantee anything in the way of tempera- ment. I often hear people talking about breeds that are wonderful family dogs; this depends greatly on the individual dog's character and the individual family.

BREED CAPABILITIES

Considering that all dogs, regardless of the breed, are born with the same traits, it would seem logical to say that all breeds are capable of doing all tasks. However, this is not the case. Not all breeds can do all jobs, for a number of reasons—primarily physical, not mental ones. For example, a Pomeranian would obviously not be able to do water rescue work the way a Newfoundland can. The Pomeranian may be as courageous and intelligent as the Newfie, but has obvious physical limitations.

However, that same Pomeranian might be well suited to do many other jobs that would seem unlikely for the breed. For example, he might be taught to pull a cart—a very, very small one, mind you. Or he could be taught to do service dog work, assisting someone who is hearing impaired by alerting them to the phone ringing or to the doorbell. Dogs' abilities are not limited by their breed, but rather by the individual dog's physical ability and character, and of course the abilities of the dog's handler.

Many dogs have missed out on showing their stuff because they have been limited by misconceptions of the dog-owning public. In the same vein, many dogs have been labeled stubborn or dumb because they haven't lived up to their breed's stereotype. People may be shocked and disappointed that their retriever isn't nuts about retrieving or that the breed everyone told them would make a great protection dog isn't very protective.

Specific abilities are developed through breeding and training.

DOG IQ

There is no denying the fact that certain breeds of dogs tend to learn certain tasks more quickly. However, within each breed you will find a wide range of intellectual capabilities. Therefore, it seems a very silly notion to rank breeds of purebred dogs in order of intelligence.

Also, keep in mind that humans have selectively bred animals to perform tasks. Some of those tasks may require an animal to think for themselves, which is surely not a sign of low intelligence. For example, the Afghan Hound was bred to hunt at a great distance ahead of its handlers, often having to make its own decisions. Today Afghans still tend to think for themselves, sometimes to the frustration of their owners. On the other hand, many of the sporting breeds assisted human hunters at a closer range and were therefore in a better position to be guided by a handler. But because they are sometimes more willing to follow commands does not mean they are more intelligent.

DO DOGS THINK?

One of the biggest problems facing owners is that they are not sure their dogs can think. Owners rarely give the dog a chance to make a decision for himself, so most dog training relies on the owner being present to actively make every decision for their dog. By doing so, you are creating a situation where you must be present in order for your dog to behave the way you want him to.

For example, if a dog goes into the garbage most owners will yell, "No, bad dog!" Relying on your voice to constantly correct your dog for inappropriate

This Dachshund will associate the act of jumping on someone with the negative consequence of the throw chain.

When he places all four feet on the ground, he will be praised for making a good choice.

behavior rarely teaches him more than that he should be cautious when you are around. But what happens when you leave him alone and he must make choices about his own behavior?

One way to give your dog a chance to think (and therefore learn) is to remove yourself from the situation, at least from the dog's perspective. If your dog has a negative experience when he sticks his nose in the garbage can (because you've set up a booby trap), he has the chance to think about the situation without worrying about you: Is it worth it to stick my nose in there? If the correction is appropriate, his answer will be no.

Making a choice between pleasure and discomfort is a thinking process. We want our dogs to think things through and learn on their own. Your dog might think through a problem this way: When I jump on people they march straight ahead (negative), but when I come to the person and stand or sit in front of him, I get praised and petted (positive). Dogs have the ability to reason. They can distinguish pleasure from discomfort. Your dog can think well enough to choose pleasure over discomfort.

STRESS AND YOUR DOG

Most people have times when they feel stressed. Our stress is usually caused by the pressures of work and family. If we sometimes feel stressed living in a society we designed and basically understand, imagine how your dog feels living in a world that is not his own.

Try to relate to how your dog is feeling when you are teaching him something new. Imagine being dropped off in a foreign country and trying to understand what people are saying to you and what they expect of you. A lot of a dog's stress comes from not knowing what is expected of him.

The process of learning is stressful. So the calmer and clearer you are when teaching your dog, the better. This means you need to remain as unemotional as possible to lessen your dog's confusion and help him learn.

Dogs often relieve their stress by being self-destructive or by destroying their environment; this is often wrongly interpreted as spite or stubbornness. Dogs don't act out of spite. Before you accuse your dog of this, ask yourself, Where did spite come from? It is a human emotion, not an animal emotion. Dogs understand survival, in which spite plays no part.

You will find that by teaching your dog the four basic commands in this book, you will have laid the foundation for him to understand his place in your world. And that is the only way he can survive in your family.

THE RIGHT DOG FOR YOU

There are an enormous number of reasons to get a dog. Among them are companionship and physical support (from a service or guide dog). Only you can decide if your reasons are right. Remember that the choice you make may lead to 10 to 15 years of emotional and financial responsibility for a living, feeling creature. It is a choice you should not make lightly.

In order to have the best chance for a long and healthy dog–human bond, the questions that follow should be asked of every person in your household before you get a dog.

IS NOW THE RIGHT TIME?

Only you can decide when the best time is for you to get a dog. However, there are some general guidelines. Holidays are rarely the right time to get any new pet, because there is too much going on for you to be able to make the pet's new environment safe and secure.

A dog should never be a surprise gift for someone. The potential owner should always be involved, to decide if it is the right time for a dog and which type of dog is best for them. Is everyone ready to spend the time a dog will need daily for its care, training and well-being? Is everyone able to make a long-term commitment?

WHAT KIND OF CHARACTER?

For most people, one of the first steps in the process of choosing a dog is writing down a list of the breeds they find most attractive or going to a shelter and picking out the dogs they consider to be the best looking. Way before you get to this point you should think about two things: What kind of lifestyle do you lead and what character in a dog would be most compatible with this lifestyle?

Do you have a temperament that would be more compatible with a dog of a softer character or a stronger character? If you answered a stronger character, that does not necessarily mean you should own a large guarding breed. Character is not measured in size. You may find that a small or medium dog with a strong character is best suited to your life.

Within each and every breed and mix of breeds you will find all types of characters. If you go out and buy breed A, for example, because you heard they are really tough dogs, you and the dog may be sorely disappointed. Don't match yourself to a breed, match yourself to the individual dog's temperament and needs. If there are several members of your household, be sure the dog is suited to them as closely as possible, as well.

WHAT AGE DOG?

There is no disputing the fact that puppies are adorable. Getting a dog when he is a very young puppy gives you the chance to establish the habits you want in your older dog. But the time and energy required to mold your puppy into a wonderful adult dog are often too much for the average person. This is one of the reasons that so many dogs end up in shelters.

There are many alternatives to bringing home an eight-week-old puppy. And yes, you can create a very strong bond with an adult dog. This is not to say that an adult dog will not require teaching and guidance in

Puppies are certainly adorable, but they can be a lot of work.

its new home. However, the time required is usually quite a bit less than a very young puppy needs.

With an adult dog, you know exactly what you're getting. There are no questions such as how big he will get or what his personality will be like. Furthermore, an adult dog is likely to have bladder and bowel control, which will greatly decrease the number of walks needed.

If you have your heart set on raising your dog from puppyhood, remember that the first 14 weeks of a dog's life have an enormous impact on his behavior as an adult. Be sure you will have the time to properly socialize the puppy during these formative weeks, and that you won't get frustrated with the enormous time commitment needed for a very young puppy. If your schedule is going to be very hectic, consider waiting until the pup is a few weeks older. Just be sure the environment where he is staying during those few weeks is enriching and healthy, both physically and mentally.

If you have found it in your heart to adopt an older dog, there are some special instructions to follow. First and foremost, you should get a crate suited for the dog. You cannot be sure of this dog's lifestyle before you adopted him, so the crate will confine him until you teach him your house rules (see Chapter Seven for more on crate training). There are times when an adult dog's history makes crate training too difficult. For example, the crate may have been used to punish the dog in his previous home. In this case, try to confine him to one room of your home when you're not there to supervise him.

In the new environment of your home it may take him time to feel comfortable, so you probably won't see his established habits for a couple of weeks. This time is often referred to as the honeymoon period.

You should also take your older dog to the vet for a checkup. A hint about house training is that even if you were told the dog is house trained, take it with a grain of salt. Even if he really is, he may make mistakes due to stress, which can cause loose stools. Stress may affect him in other ways as well. He may panic when left alone and be destructive in many ways. Before he has the run of the house you need to make sure he knows the rules while you are around to watch him. A crate will help you control his behavior when you're not around.

WHAT SIZE?

The size of a dog at maturity is a serious consideration. All too often people choose a cute little puppy without recognizing that he or she will grow into a 90-pound adult. Also, when researching a breed remember that you should look at the adult relatives of a prospective puppy, because even within a breed there can be an amazing range of sizes.

WHAT ABOUT THE HAIR?

The type of coat the dog has will affect the amount of time you will need to spend on grooming. While all

Dogs come in an amazing range of sizes.

The coat of the Portuguese Water Dog on the left will require more care than the coat of the Labrador Retriever on the right. However, both dogs require the same attention regarding the care of their teeth, nails and ears.

dogs, regardless of coat type, require basic grooming care such as brushing, cleaning teeth and clipping nails, a Greyhound needs a lot less care than an Old English Sheepdog in full coat.

WHAT SHOULD YOUR DOG LOOK LIKE?

While we certainly don't recommend ever thinking of your dog as a fashion accessory, this is still an important question. However, it is often the question on the *top* of people's list, which is one of the main reasons why so many dog–human matches don't work and the dog ultimately ends up abandoned.

Appreciating your dog's physical attributes is one of the joys of dog ownership. If you have a preference for a certain color or style of dog, then use that to narrow down the list of dogs you have come up with that are generally suitable in other ways, such as temperament, size, grooming needs and exercise requirements.

MALE OR FEMALE?

There are many myths associated with the sex of dogs. The major one is that females are sweeter than males. Again, the temperament of your dog will be due to many things, and of course the animal's sex plays a part. However, many people get themselves in trouble by choosing a dog because of its sex when there are many other factors that are much more important.

There may be five males and three females in a litter you are choosing your puppy from. Don't dis-count the fact that the puppy with the most compatible personality may be one of the males, even if you were told by friends that you should only look at the females.

Some of the problems associated with males, such as marking territory, can be greatly reduced by neutering the dog, and by not allowing these habits to become established in the first place. For females, the twice yearly heats can be eliminated by spaying.

ARE THERE POTENTIAL GENETIC DEFECTS?

If you are interested in a specific breed, check out the known potential genetic defects common to that breed and the breeders' efforts to breed for animals that are free of those problems. A conscientious breeder will have all their sires and dams tested for genetic problems, and can show you the papers that certify their dogs are clear of problems.

This is the best a breeder can do, but even that may not be enough. Sometimes genetic defects are hidden in recessive genes that do not express themselves in the parents but may show up in the offspring. The further back you go in a dog's pedigree, the more you are likely to know about the dog's genetic heritage. Talk to your dog's breeder about this.

WHERE TO FIND A DOG?

Shelters Obviously, adopting a dog from a shelter can be a very rewarding experience. When choosing a dog, many shelters will offer an evaluation of the dog's temperament. Even with this evaluation you should try to spend as much time with the dog as possible. Bring your whole household but try not to have everyone petting the dog at the same time, as it is too stressful for the dog.

Take him for a walk and a mini-training session on the shelter grounds. Does he pull? How is he around other animals? How is he around toys and food? How is his general obedience? What does he seem to be afraid of? Obviously, any animal in a shelter is under enormous stress and it is impossible to get a truly accurate picture of his temperament. But it is better to at least make an effort than to choose him solely because he looks cute.

Rescue Groups Rescue groups are organizations that focus on rescuing dogs, usually purebreds, from shelters, the street or unsuitable homes. If you are interested in owning a purebred dog, buying one from a breeder is not your only option. You can obtain the breed of your choice and at the same time adopt an animal who is in need of a home. Homeless dogs are often stigmatized as having something wrong with them. But more often than not this isn't the case. Dogs are given up for a variety of reasons, including divorce and the death of an owner.

Every breed of purebred dog has at least one rescue group in this country, and some have as many as 20 or 30 local groups. They are run by volunteers who have a true love of and commitment to a particular breed and devote many hours (and dollars) to aiding dogs in need.

Animals available through rescue groups range in age from very young puppies to elderly dogs. Before being placed in a new home, each dog is evaluated for mental and physical soundness. In many cases the dog's history is available, such as if he has been raised with children, if he is comfortable with other animals and what sort of training he has received.

For more information on breed rescue groups, contact the American Kennel Club at (919) 233-9767. Rescue contact names are also available from the AKC's site on the World Wide Web at http://www.akc.org.

Breeders A reputable breeder of purebred dogs is most interested in furthering the best interests of the breed she is involved in. This means she wants to breed dogs that come as close as possible to the mental and physical ideal of the breed, as stated in the breed standard.

It is rare that a good breeder makes any money by breeding dogs. In fact, she would be lucky to break even. An enormous amount of time and money is spent on properly feeding and housing the dogs, on testing for any potential genetic defects, on veterinary support for the dam and her puppies and on traveling to dog shows. After all of this effort, you should expect such a person to be very concerned about the quality of the homes where she places her puppies. So don't be surprised if she asks you as many questions as you ask her.

Ask the breeder if she tests for genetic disorders common to the breed. By routinely testing breeding stock for genetic disorders, breeders can decrease the chance that they will be producing inferior stock. Ask her what disorders she tests her dogs for and ask to see the test certification.

Find out what her priorities are in her breeding program. A breeder's top priorities should be temperament and health. Is she breeding for dogs who will be successful show dogs? Is she also concerned that the dogs be able to carry out the tasks they were designed to do? For example, there are many sporting dogs being bred who have very little inclination to carry out hunting tasks. You want a dog who is bred as much (if not more) for his brains as for his looks.

If you are buying a purebred dog from a reputable breeder, you should spend some time with the dam and, if possible, the sire of the litter. They should both look healthy, and their surroundings should be well kept. It is important that they be good examples of their breed physically, but even more important, they should be the kind of dogs you would want to live with. There is no disputing the fact that genetics play a part in the character of a dog, so the temperament of a puppy's relatives can be a good indicator of what your puppy's temperament will be like. One of the most accurate ways to get an idea of what your puppy's adult personality will be like is to look at adults from previous litters of the same mating, if possible.

You can find reputable breeders by inquiring with the American Kennel Club or local breed or training clubs, and by attending dog shows.

PUPPY TESTING

There is no scientific way to measure the accuracy of puppy temperament tests, but there is certainly no harm in testing. However, the traditional tests, such as pinching a puppy's toes to see how touch sensitive he is or restraining him to see his response, are not that likely to give you any meaningful information and are more likely to stress the puppy. A mini-training session is more likely to reveal at least a little something about the match between the dog's character and your own. And if possible, you should try to visit the puppies more than once, to get a better idea of their general character.

Puppies are more comfortable in a familiar environment, so it is best to test a puppy *before* you take him to your home, where his behavior will probably be rather cautious for the first week or so.

If there are kids in your household, take them with you to look at the puppies, and choose one or two of the pups you are most attracted to. You should take the puppies aside, away from the litter, because they already have an established relationship with their pack and you want to see what they are like on their own. One at a time let them interact with one of the children and the rest of the family.

Do a little training test. When the puppy tries to jump on the child, gently replace him into a Sit. See how many times it takes for him to pause and reconsider jumping on the child. Then try another puppy. This may give you an indication of the pup's basic learning capacity. You can also give a toy to the puppy and then take it away. Compare each puppy's reaction when an object is taken from him.

One of the biggest mistakes people make when choosing a puppy from a litter is to take the one that seems the most outgoing. Often that puppy has a very strong character and is not always suited to the average pet home. After spending some time with a litter, you may find that a puppy with a character more in the middle range is best suited for you.

Remember, there is no one perfect puppy, but there is such a thing as a perfect match. You're choosing a household companion for the next decade or more, so take your time and choose carefully.

CHOOSING TO BEHAVE RIGHT

Just as you would never think of neglecting your child's education, you must educate your dog. It is your job to explain to your dog how he should behave in your world. Expect your dog to behave like a dog—this includes eliminating when and where he feels the need to, chewing, barking and digging—unless you teach him otherwise. The laws dogs are born to follow are very different from the laws pet owners expect them to follow.

The reasons for *not* teaching a dog how to behave in our world are numerous. Some people say they just don't have the time, some don't know how, and our personal favorite is the owner who says, "I just want him to be able to be a dog." In that case, let him live in the wild, because a dog who is "just" a dog has no place in our world. It is inhumane to leave a dog in a state of confusion about the rules of our world. Most dogs in this predicament end up doing something that costs them their life: behaving unmanageably, biting someone or getting hit by a car.

Training should not inhibit a dog's playfulness or spirit. The laws of our own society don't have to make our lives dull, do they? Actually, once you have taught your dog what is expected of him, he can be allowed more freedom to interact safely and enjoyably in the human world.

In this chapter you will learn how to lay the groundwork for teaching your dog the four basic commands that make up the foundation of your dog's training: Sit, Down, Come and Release. I also will give you some suggestions on how to use these commands to help your dog fit into your family's lifestyle. After a few months of lifestyle training, the positive behaviors you have taught your dog will become the habits of a lifetime.

Too many people attempt to teach their dog basic commands, such as Sit and Down, but don't use them in real life, except as tricks to show their friends. Then, when the dog behaves inappropriately, they are more concerned with punishing the dog than using the training to show the dog what behaviors are appropriate. A great example of this is when your dog jumps on you. Instead of yelling at him to get off, use the word Sit to teach him how to greet people.

The purpose of teaching the basic commands is to make your life with your dog more enjoyable for both of you. It would be unfair for any trainer to tell you how you should live with your dog. It is your place to decide how you want to use the foundation training in your life. If you are having specific behavioral problems with your dog, such as aggression or fearfulness, refer to Chapter Eight. Under those circumstances you will want to follow a more rigidly defined program in order to see results.

TRAINING THEORIES

There are many ways in which dogs, people and in fact, all animals can learn. Some of these learning methods have been adopted by animal trainers. Let's take a look at a few.

Heuristic This method is often used by science teachers in the biology or chemistry lab. Students are given a hypothesis and a way to test it. The information they learn is easy to remember because they are involved in the entire process and observe the results for themselves. The teacher is merely there as a facilitator to provide encouragement and to ask questions designed to make the students think. When the students succeed, the teacher expresses delight in their scientific discovery. As a result, the students learn the information and are able to apply it to many other situations.

This method is promoted in this book. We believe it is the most humane and effective method of training your dog.

Didactic This is the most common method of teaching both animals and people. The teacher tells the information to the students and expects them to remember it. Not surprisingly, students often forget the information because their critical thinking skills are not involved. Often, even the students who are able to perform well on tests are unable to apply the information to any practical situation.

It is this didactic method that dog trainers have traditionally promoted. The trainer tries to teach the dog a command, using the threat of a verbal and/or physical reprimand if the dog disobeys. Actually, the disobedience usually represents confusion on the dog's part. This process does not give the dog the opportunity to figure out the problem; rather, it focuses his thinking on the reprimand coming from the trainer.

Lure and Reward Training With this method the dog is lured into a position using a bit of food or a favorite toy. He receives the reward when he completes the task. The reward is originally given every time the task is completed, then intermittently, to keep the dog guessing when he will receive the next reward. The main problem with this method is that it

The owner is attempting to instruct her English Springer Spaniel by verbally reprimanding him for breaking a Down command. The dog is focused on his owner's emotions, which means he can't be focused on learning what the command means.

can make the dog too anxious to get to the end of task. We want our dogs to enjoy executing our commands, not the end of them.

One of the other problems with this method of training is that dogs, by nature, will voluntarily submit to receive something. So you can't be really sure whether you are teaching a new concept or reinforcing a natural submissive behavior. For example, a mother dog might carry food back to her puppies, who sit or lie down in front of her to encourage her to give them food. They have not learned a Sit or a Down, but have simply learned that acting submissive gets them more food.

Furthermore, many people are not skilled at appropriately randomizing rewards and get locked into a situation where the dog only listens to a command when a reward or lure is offered. It is a good idea to teach the commands first, then use food as a bonus once the dog understands he must do it because you said so.

Fabian lures this puppy into a Sit using a piece of food in his hand. Many dogs trained using this method learn the word Sit means do so only if a treat is offered.

WHAT MAKES TRAINING WORK?

Your dog's training is limited by two things: your effort and his physical capabilities, in terms of both health and conformation.

How you approach training your dog will have an enormous effect on your success. You should see this as an opportunity to teach your dog how to become a happy canine citizen. The only thing you need to worry about is making sure your dog does not see if you get frustrated or angry at him. Anger has no place in the teaching process. This will only confuse him. Remain as neutral as possible, unless you are offering praise. Your voice should never be used to punish or correct your dog, only to tell him what is expected of him and to praise him for doing it.

Praise is one of the most effective training tools any owner can possess. You can praise your dog using your voice, your hands and your attention. Use praise often in training to let your dog know what you like. Don't ignore or take good behavior for granted. The majority of training time should be spent praising while the dog is on commands—teaching that even though the command is the law it is still a pleasurable thing to do.

With praise, timing is everything. In order for praise to be associated with a particular behavior, it must occur at the same time as the behavior. Praise your dog at the *exact* moment you are pleased with his behavior.

Here is an example of the misuse of praise: You ask your dog to Sit. He obeys and stays there waiting for you to release him or to give him another command. During this time you are silent, maybe for fear that if you make a sound your dog will break his Sit. After a few moments you release the dog and then (finally) you praise him profusely. What has the dog been praised for in this situation? He was praised when he was released from the command. Praising at this time will only teach the dog to anticipate being released from the Sit. Do you really want to praise your dog for getting up from a Sit? Instead, praise the dog during the act of sitting—after all, isn't that what you wanted?

When you time it right, praise is the reward given for the act of obeying the command. Your dog will even begin to see your request for a Sit or a Down as praise because you are giving the dog another chance to be right.

You can tailor your praise to your dog. If you have a dog who is very active, for instance, you may want to tone down your praise slightly, especially during the foundation training described in the next chapter. When you are sure your dog understands the whole concept of each command, then you should be able to praise in almost any way you want. But be sure praise is accomplishing what it is intended to. It is meant to let your dog know that what he is doing is the right thing. So if you have a dog with a softer character, wild, rough praise might make him uncomfortable and be viewed as more of a negative than a positive.

USING CORRECTIONS

It is unlikely that an animal would consistently behave in a certain way solely for the purpose of receiving rewards. A dog's behavior is also guided by the desire to avoid undesirable experiences (as is ours). If given a fair chance, a dog will avoid unpleasantness, so correction should play a limited part in an effective and humane training program.

Corrections are more often than not physical when training dogs. This is because we cannot talk to dogs the way we can talk to each other, to explain what we think they have done wrong.

This owner is confusing her dog by showing him how frustrated she is with him for getting up from a Down. She has made herself part of the correction by making direct eye contact with her dog and through her body language.

In reality, even with people there are times when we need to experience mild physical discomfort before we learn. For example, almost all small children are told many times to stay away from a hot stove top. Inevitably, one day the child is unattended for a moment and reaches to touch the stove. It is unfortunate that almost all of us have been burned in this way, but one correction from the stove is usually all we need to learn to steer clear of it.

If a dog in the wild chose to pester a porcupine, he would get a physical correction. While nobody likes to see any animal in discomfort, the correction given by the porcupine is extremely effective because it will usually take only one correction to teach the dog to

In the dog's mind, this correction is as disconnected from Fabian as possible because Fabian is not letting the dog see his emotions.

stay away from porcupines. Dogs need to know the negative is there but should not have to live with the negative all the time. We want them to live with the positive.

To start, corrections play no part in training until you have taught the dog the right behavior. Just as we

expect to be told about a new law before we are arrested for breaking it, so your dog should be taught the rules you have devised before he receives any corrections. Once you know he understands the rules, then correction may play a part in enforcing those rules.

Just as with praise, for a correction to be associated with a particular behavior it must occur at the same time as the behavior. You can't explain to a dog that they are being punished for something they did five minutes ago. This misconception is most often applied when owners walk in the front door to find the dog has chewed a piece of furniture or has eliminated in the house. They proceed to drag the dog to the site of the offense and verbally or physically punish him. What a waste of your dog's trust! All he learns from experiences like this is that you are sometimes so furious when you walk in the front door that he'd better cringe and act as submissive as possible in order to avoid your wrath.

One of the most important things about corrections is that they remain unemotional and disconnected from the people giving them. Corrections should, from the dog's point of view, come from the environment, not from you. This means when you administer a correction you should not speak to the dog or make eye contact. In this way your dog will understand clearly that the correction comes from the unwanted behavior, not from you.

Corrections should never be verbal, because when you use your voice to make corrections you are inevitably including some level of anger or displeasure. You can't detach yourself when you give verbal reprimands, even gentle ones such as "Aaargh" or "Ep, ep." And if your dog doesn't respond to a verbal reprimand, you will inevitably try escalating it—and your anger. If you are thinking, "But I want my dog to know I am mad at him sometimes," consider this: If you teach him not to do things because you might get mad at him, he will most likely just choose to do the things when you aren't around. This is very logical thinking on the part of your dog. Sadly, it is this sort of thinking that gets dogs labeled as stubborn and spiteful. You want to train the dog to behave appropriately whether or not you are there. So leave yourself out of the corrections and your dog will always see you as the good guy.

Corrections should not be repetitive. If you must use the same correction over and over and it is not causing a change in the dog's behavior, you should try something else. Most people monotonously repeat corrections, most often jerking on the leash to stop the dog from pulling, in the hopes that at some point the dog will get so sick of it that he will obey. If the correction for speeding down the highway doing 80 miles an hour was a fine of one dollar, how many people would slow down to avoid the fine? Not many! How long do you think it would take for state officials to raise the fine? Not long! This does not mean you should escalate the level of the correction. Instead, try a different correction—one the dog has not learned how to tune out.

USING REWARDS AND CORRECTIONS

It is only fair to make it as clear as possible to your dog what the criteria are for both rewards and corrections. Otherwise he will be confused and most likely receive more corrections than he should. If you expect your dog to sit the first time you say it, then you must stick with that rule. If you change the criteria one day and let him slide, you will be setting up a situation where the next time he may disobey when you really want him to comply. So you will harshly correct him when the day before you allowed him to disobey. It is obvious how unfair this is to the dog.

You must keep praise and corrections clearly separated in order to maintain the value of both as training tools. Do not devalue praise by muddying it with corrections. We often see clients return to correct a dog who has gotten up from a Sit or a Down and reach in to snap the lead with one hand, only to reach in with the other almost simultaneously to pet the dog when back in position. From the dog's point of view it may be unclear whether breaking a command brought about a correction or just brought the owner over for a nice pat on the head.

Praise and correction can be confused in another way, too. It is often the case that the owner's idea of a correction is the dog's idea of a reward. For example, if you are watching television and your dog decides he wants your attention, he may start to whine or bark to get it. In response, you may yell at the dog to be quiet. In this case, you understandably view a verbal reprimand as an appropriate correction. However, the dog's original intent was to get your attention focused on him and that is exactly what happened. So you have, in effect, rewarded the dog for vocalizing and have taught him that it is a way to get your attention.

Learning happens when a dog associates a behavior or act with a consequence. That consequence may be considered by the dog to be positive or negative. The perception of the consequence determines the likelihood the behavior will increase or decrease. If the consequence is perceived as a positive (for example, the dog rummages through the garbage and finds a steak), it is likely he will perform that behavior again. If the consequence is perceived as a negative (for example, the dog rummages through the garbage, hears a loud noise and feels an object hit his rump), he is less likely to perform that behavior again.

FRACTURE

Most people who have owned a dog for more than three months have developed a strong relationship with their dog. Both dog and owner probably have a lot of habits and patterns of behavior that don't benefit the dog-human relationship. You may be sending confusing signals about what you expect from your dog, and he may be acting too much like a dog in your human world.

Experience, knowledge and a good sense of timing play a part in the success of a professional trainer's ability to train dogs. However, even a mildly competent trainer will probably have more success with a dog than that dog's owner. The reason is that the trainer is starting fresh with the dog. There is no established history between the dog and trainer. So the trainer has the opportunity to make her voice very powerful to the dog (not in tone or volume, but in meaning). The very first time the trainer gives a command, she also enforces it. She never allows an opportunity for the dog to build a history of non-compliance.

Creating a fracture also means giving you and your dog the opportunity to start with a clean slate—to forget the patterns of behavior that caused conflicts between you. It is like starting over with a brand new puppy, except that you will start over with your dog at any age. You as the owner need to wipe the slate clean before any real training can possibly work.

One of the best ways to create a fracture is to go someplace the dog hasn't been before. This neutral place, with no history of inappropriate habits, will be the first step in the fracture. This new environment will give you an edge over your dog. He will be more likely to be slightly uncomfortable and dependent on you to see him through.

The most important thing is that you use this new environment as a tool to gain a new power in your voice. You will gain this power by enforcing commands from the very first time you say them.

When Fabian sees the dog is distracted, he will snap the leash. The moment the dog turns to pay attention to him, Fabian will praise and encourage him to come closer. Notice the line tied to the ground stake, which offers added control.

Don't say anything until you are absolutely ready to enforce it. After you gain control in this neutral place, that control will then be transferred to the areas where the dog's bad habits were established.

How do you create this fracture? It all begins with attention. Without attention you can't do any training that will have any long-term effect. You may be able to get your dog to Sit or Down for a moment, but you will be unable to teach him the full meaning of these commands.

You want to teach your dog that there is nobody he can depend on more than you. He must always look to you for direction. There is nothing wrong with expecting your dog's attention—it's for his safety. The way we teach him to do this is by showing him that you are a safe zone and corrections come from the environment outside of you. He'll see the world as a mine field—the corrections are mines—but if he pays attention to you, you'll direct him safely through them.

It is essential when you are attempting to create a fracture that you remain as unemotional as possible. It is fair to say that most owners are very emotional with their dogs, in both praising and reprimanding them. This is your chance to make your dog see you

Another form of correction is a throw object, in this case a chain. It is tossed at the dog's flank only when he is facing away from the handler.

There are three ways to create a fracture with your dog: Using two leash lines, one line or a crate. Using two lines is the easiest way. The first should be 20 to 30 feet long. This is the anchor line, used to keep the dog within a circular boundary and to bring him in to you if he gets confused. Attach this to a tree or a ground stake. The second line is your control line and should be about half the length of the anchor line.

Now, using the control line, walk around with your dog. Your top priority in this process is to avoid your dog. You should actually try to lose his attention, because only by losing it will you be able to help him understand why he shouldn't lose sight of you. Your dog's top priority is to pay attention to you. You want to get him thinking that he'd better watch you because he never knows which way you are going and you might walk away or right into him.

There are three corrections that can be used in the fracture process. Usually you should start with a leash correction, which is just a tug on the leash. The second correction is a small bean bag and the third is a throw chain (for more on these training tools, see Chapter Six). You will throw the bean bag and chain at the dog's rump, aiming to startle but not hurt him.

When the dog is distracted and is facing away from you, snap the leash. When he turns to look, act as though you don't know how the leash snap happened and encourage him to come to you, the safe zone.

Mix up the corrections, tossing either the bean bag or the throw chain at his rump area when he isn't

in a totally different light. So start by changing the way you interact with your dog. Save the power of your voice to be used only when you are praising or giving a command—never a correction.

This Bulldog puppy was brought into the situation as a strong distraction for the German Shepherd. The Shepherd must understand that paying attention to Fabian is the best thing for her, regardless of what's happening in her environment.

looking at you. It is imperative that you do this when the dog can't see you tossing anything and that you do not add any verbal signals with this or any correction. You want the dog to think these objects drop on his rear out of the sky when he isn't paying attention to you.

You shouldn't have to make too many corrections before your dog starts to understand what you are teaching him. If he focuses on you it means positive things will happen (praise). If he focuses elsewhere it means negative things will happen.

Now you're ready to test your dog's understanding of the concept of paying attention by setting up distractions. These could be adults walking by, children or another dog. When your dog has learned to focus mainly on you even with distractions, it's time to test him in a new environment.

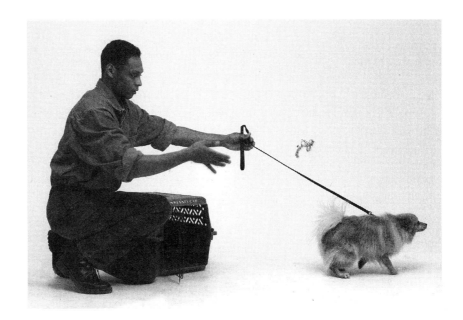

This Pomeranian, Molly, was completely distracted from Fabian.

Molly is learning that paying attention to Fabian is the best way to avoid negatives and receive positives. When she focuses on him, he uses his voice to praise and encourage her.

By "focused on you" I don't mean that your dog's eyes should be glued to you at all times. Of course dogs look around them and notice their environment. What you should look for is repeated glances toward you. Wherever you move, at the very least your dog should indicate that he sees you moving. When you have accomplished this, you will have developed a handler-centric dog. This is a dog that notices you even in the absence of a command. Your dog should feel that paying attention to you, or being centered on you, is the best way to ensure he is safe.

You can go through the whole fracture process using just one leash. However, you may find that you don't have as much control. If you choose to create a fracture in this way, you should be sure to do a lot of left turns to get your dog's attention focused on you. You should also probably switch collars, meaning if you have been using a flat collar try a slip collar and if you have been using a slip you might try a pinch collar (see Chapter Six for more on choosing a collar). Generally speaking, a new type of collar is necessary in order to have some impact on the dog. If the dog has been pulling on a slip collar for the last two or three months, the effectiveness of a correction on that collar is probably minimal.

Shape the dog's behavior to focus on you the same way as explained for the two-line method, but remember you will probably find that you have a little less control at first because the dog isn't anchored.

If you want to create a fracture at home, it's a little more difficult but definitely possible. To do so you will need to crate your dog. The idea is to teach him to focus on you every time you take him out of the crate. You will get his attention in much the same way as you would outside, using the same three methods of correction. Let your dog get distracted, and when he does, use one of the three methods to refocus his attention on you.

TRAINING HAPPENS EVERYWHERE

You may have taught your dog what certain words mean, but don't be surprised when he tries to figure out if the words mean the same thing everywhere. Does Sit mean Sit at the vet's office? Does Down mean Down when there is a party at home? Don't get upset and say, "He already knows this, he's just being stubborn." The way your dog behaves is not stubbornness, it's part of the learning process. Just calmly enforce the commands so that he knows they apply everywhere.

It might be helpful to you and your dog if you pretend the dog knows no commands. Starting from scratch may help you to be less emotional during the training process. This way you won't be constantly telling yourself, "He already knows this!"

By you consistently enforcing commands, he will learn that they always mean the same thing, regardless of where he is or what is going on. Remember, your dog's behavior is formed every day, 24 hours a day. This is why you must use real life to train your dog. If someone wants to say hello to your dog, use that moment to reinforce the habit of sitting to greet people.

One of the times people forget to train their dogs is during play sessions. Use play time to test how well your dog knows what you're saying. Right in the middle of play, stop what you are doing and give your dog a command. He must obey, even if he is very excited. If you think this is unfair, imagine that your dog is chasing a ball and is about to run out in front of a car to get it; you'll be glad he knows that he must obey commands even in the middle of a play session, even when he's excited.

WHY SHOULD YOUR DOG OBEY COMMANDS?

Dogs do not obey commands out of devotion or loyalty to humans. The image of Lassie and many other celebrity dogs has done a great disservice to dogs. Many people come to us believing their dog is a

This Bulldog, Winston, is going to be expected to greet people in a calm manner as an adult, so he is being shown how to do so as a puppy. Notice that the children have been instructed to be fair and calm with Winston.

"lemon" because he doesn't care about being loyal to them and making them happy.

Dogs have no idea what is good and bad in human terms. If your dog is behaving in a manner that you find is inappropriate, it is simply because he has not been made to understand that such actions result in a negative consequence for him. Trying to teach your dog to obey in order to avoid making you angry is foolish and ineffective.

A good example of this is the garbage raiding dog. Many owners yell at their dog every time they catch him with his nose in the garbage. The owners don't understand why their dog keeps doing it when the dog "knows" it makes them angry. The dog does it because rummaging in the garbage is a rewarding experience. While being yelled at is considered by most dogs to be a negative, they quickly figure out that rummaging in the garbage doesn't cause the yelling—being caught does. So they learn to rummage when you aren't around. Your dog would avoid garbage cans like the plague if they caused him discomfort whenever he stuck his nose in them, whether you were there or not.

Your dog will obey you and the rules you consistently set down if he learns that doing so benefits his welfare. You are teaching the dog that commands and rules are positive—even though it is the law for him to obey, it is still a pleasurable thing to do.

It is often difficult for owners to see good results when training their dogs, but the reason for this has nothing to do with the dog being disloyal or unloving or stubborn. It has more to do with the fact that the dog has an established relationship with the owner that has muddied the learning process. The owner and dog have a history that is usually emotional and confusing. For example, the owner may have gotten into the habit of saying Sit many times in a row to the dog. When the dog doesn't respond the owner may give up out of frustration or simply label the dog as stubborn or believe the dog doesn't care enough about him to obey. The owner now has a lot of negative feelings about the dog and the dog has learned that the word Sit means very little. This is where the fracture comes into play. You must give yourself and your dog a chance to start fresh.

FOUNDATION TRAINING

The four foundation commands your dog will learn in this chapter—Sit, Down, Come and Release—are enough for just about anyone to train their dog to fit into their life. This is the foundation training for everything else your dog needs to know. How you use these four foundation commands will determine your dog's lifestyle.

There are various levels at which you can expect your dog to perform the four foundation commands. When you walk down the street you definitely want your dog to walk politely without pulling on his leash. But do you want him to walk a foot away from you and glance at you every five to six steps? Or would you prefer your dog to be able to walk three feet or so away and only occasionally glance at you? Most owners don't want regimented marching (this is usually reserved for competitive Obedience), but some dogs may require this level of control.

Your dog's character and established habits play a part in determining the level of performance you

choose. A dog who has been allowed to establish the habit of lunging at other dogs on the street might have to be walked in a more controlled manner than a dog who doesn't have this habit.

Chosen levels have to be maintained—the higher the level, the more maintenance and responsibility, so you need to decide what level your lifestyle needs and if you'll stick with it. An obedient dog is the dog you feel fits comfortably into your lifestyle, not what a trainer says it is. The only way it will work is if you are satisfied, because you have to live with the dog and maintain its training day to day.

Owners often let the level of training go down and then expect it to go back up. This is unfair and confusing to the dog. If two out of 10 times you let the dog ignore a command, you have to expect that the meaning of the command is going to change for the dog. Come will no longer mean turn and run to you; it will mean something more like, if you feel like it and nothing more interesting is going on, turn and

For this mixed breed, Come means to walk somewhere near his owner, as long as the leash is slack.

For this Labrador Retriever, Come means to stay pretty close to his owner's side with a slack leash.

This Gordon Setter understands that Come means to pay complete attention to his owner.

run to your owner. This is not so much about discipline as about expectations. If you waiver in your expectations, you will be setting your dog up to get unnecessary corrections.

You'll notice Stay is not one of the four foundation commands. Stay is a repetitive, and therefore useless, command. When you tell your dog Sit or Down, it means do it until you tell him to do something else or until you release him from the command. So there is no need for a stay command.

The word "no" also has no place in dog training. It does a great disservice to dogs and owners. The whole concept of involving yourself with the correction, with the negative, is wrong. We want the dog to see us in terms of black and white, not gray. You are always positive—he should never hear your voice and have any doubt in his mind about whether it is good or bad.

REAL-LIFE TRAINING

In teaching the four basic commands of foundation training, try to create situations that are as close to real life as possible. In real life when you place your dog on a Down it is unlikely that you will do so facing him at the end of a six-foot leash, so don't do so in foundation training. If you want to train

This is the traditional way to teach a dog to stay. In real life you don't want to have to stand in front of your dog with a raised hand to remind him to stay, so why would you teach him this way in training?

when you need them and where you need them. I call this lifestyle training.

Too many owners say their dog is perfect when they train him, but "he's still jumping on visitors." Obedience commands are taught to facilitate communication between you and your dog. Use the commands to tell your dog what it is he should do to make him right, rather than worrying about scolding your dog when he's wrong. For example, instead of yelling at him for jumping on people, tell him to Sit to greet people and help him to do so by praising him when he does. If you are reading the newspaper and he is demanding your attention, tell him to Down at your side and step on the leash so he will correct himself if he gets up. When you go to the veterinarian, use the commands you have taught your dog to keep him under your control in the waiting area and in the examination room. Integrate training into your life. You are training your dog every moment you spend with him, whether you realize it or not.

After a period of time (usually a few months), the way you use the foundation commands in your lifestyle training will become habit for your dog. If you are consistent in making him sit to greet people, he will begin to do so on his own out of habit. If you place him on a Down for five or 10 minutes every time you both come in from a walk, he will begin to do so automatically out of habit. This is when you will

to use commands for real life, do it right from the start.

Don't make the mistake of setting up training sessions for your dog after you have finished the foundation training. Remember, training is for real life, so training your dog in scheduled sessions will benefit you very little. Give commands throughout the day,

By placing the dog at his side on a Down and stepping on the leash for control, this man is helping his dog get into the habit of relaxing when he sees his owner sitting in a chair.

It is important to remind your dog that being on a command is pleasurable.

This dog lies down on his blanket out of habit when his owner sits to read a magazine because he was consistently told to do so.

truly feel that you have trained your dog to fit into your life.

A LITTLE HELP

Having one or more people assist you in training your dog will make things easier for all involved. If two people work with one dog, then one of you can go in to place the dog in position again and the other person is free to only give commands and praise. This will lessen your frustration and will clarify for the dog that commands can be enforced by many means.

Your dog should be willing to take direction from as many household members as possible. Having your household act as a training team will make it easier and more fun for you and your dog.

If you choose to have people help you in training, be sure your dog accepts those people and that they clearly understand your instructions.

Andrea placed this dog in a Down, but Fabian is replacing him. In this way Andrea's only job is to give the command and praise.

USING THE LEASH

You should hold the leash whichever way makes you feel most comfortable. However, when it comes to control and comfort we have found that one way seems to be very effective for most people. If you choose to walk your dog on your left side, you will place the end of the leash over your thumb on your left hand and grasp about six inches down from the handle so you make a loop. Then place your left hand about eight or nine inches from your right hand and relax your arms. Once your dog is in the habit of walking politely at your side, you should be able to hold the leash any way you choose and have the same ease of control.

Your dog must obey commands on leash, while being tempted by the most interesting distractions you

The end of the leash is placed over your thumb.

Make a loop with the leash by placing the hand holding the end approximately six inches down the leash. Place your other hand eight or nine inches from that.

Relax both arms down and to your side.

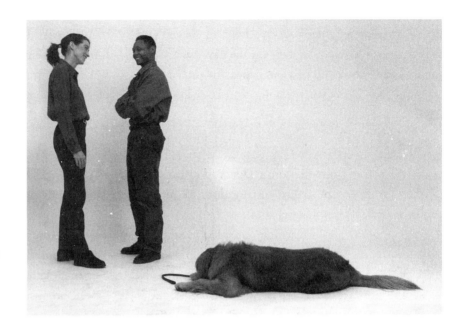

This dog was placed on a Down. If he breaks the command before he is released, Andrea or Fabian must be willing to stop the conversation and replace and/or correct him.

can possibly think of, before you should even consider teaching off-leash control. If your dog is a fanatic for hot dogs, he must understand Down means the same thing whether a person is 10 feet away reading a magazine or one foot away dangling a hot dog. If he is not as close to perfect on leash as you can expect (no dog or person is ever 100 percent), you should be cautious about taking off the leash outdoors.

COMMANDS

Choose and use your command words carefully. Only Sit can mean Sit, and only Down can mean Down. If you start changing or adding words, it is unfair to expect your dog to know you have done so and obey

the new commands. So, no more commands like sit down, get down or come over here.

Clearly define what your commands mean: Sit means put your bottom on the ground until I give you the next command or release you. Down means place your belly on the ground exactly where you are until I give you another command or release you.

How should you give a command? The answer is, just about any way you want. Just be sure your dog can hear you and that your voice isn't so loud that you scare the dog. It is silly to think you must say a command in a certain tone of voice for your dog to obey. You are teaching him the meaning of a word, not the meaning of a tone of voice. If you teach your dog to lie down only when you say Down in a deep and booming voice, what happens on the day you are in a really good mood and just can't speak in such a military fashion? Don't worry about tone; your job is just to teach the word.

Be aware that you should not give a command unless you can enforce it. If you are talking to a friend and you placed your dog on a Down, you must be willing to interrupt your conversation to replace (and/or correct) him if he gets up.

Don't worry about teaching your dog to respond to hand signals. Dogs are visually oriented and therefore pick up on motion and movement very easily. Learning words is the hard part, and usually the more important because you are going to talk to your dog more than you are going to signal him.

As you go through the motions of placing and positioning your dog, he will automatically pick up on your body language and hand signals. For instance, while you guide the leash down in the Down command, he will pick up the downward motion of your hand as a cue in addition to your voice.

THE RELEASE

When you place your dog on one of the three basic commands—Sit, Down or Come—you must have a way of telling him when he is released from the command. Otherwise, you would be leaving it up to him to decide how long a command should last.

We generally use the word Okay, but some people find they use it too frequently in their daily conversations. This might be confusing to your dog. If you place him on a Down while you are talking to a friend and in the conversation you say "okay," your dog might think you have released him.

Another phrase that is commonly used as a release is All Done. The phrase doesn't matter as long as you choose only one and stick with it.

You must teach your dog the meaning of your release word. When you want to release him from a command, say the release word and gently help your dog into a stand. This is the one command that you can repeat, because it isn't as important as the others. If your dog is hesitant to move, just take a step or two with him. For at least the first 10 or 20 times you say it, you will probably need to actually lift or encourage the dog up from a command after you say this word.

Try not to get too enthusiastic when you release your dog. Save all of the praise and excitement for when he is on a command. We want him to associate the positives coming from you with being on commands, not being released from them.

SIT

As we mentioned before, Sit means the dog must place his bottom on the ground and not move from the spot unless he's told to do something else or is released. However, if the dog lies down it is all right, because we want to be fair. Why would we need him to sit for

Apply pressure to the rear pressure points and at the same time gently lift up and slightly back on the collar.

Give the Sit command as the dog is dropping into position.

more than a minute? He is learning to stay where we put him no matter what position, Sit or Down. There's nothing wrong with letting him get comfortable.

There are several ways to place a dog in a Sit, depending on the size and character of the dog. Placement should not be a struggle. If you try one method and it takes more than seven seconds to get the dog into position, try another method.

With each method say the command word Sit as the dog is going into the position. If you say it as you

begin to try a method, you might find yourself giving the command when you are struggling with your dog, not when he is in the act of sitting. That will only create negative associations with Sit.

Whichever method you use, be sure that from the very first time the dog is put in a Sit you keep him there by gently massaging his rear and keeping your hand on his chest. You don't want him thinking that Sit means to place your bottom on the ground and pop it right back up. Also, massaging the dog's rear will help him to understand what a good place Sit is

If you raise the collar higher on the dog's neck you can apply less pressure on his rear points.

Gently cup the dog's rear and apply pressure up and slightly back on the collar.

for him. You will help your dog this way for the first five to 10 placements.

One way to teach Sit is the pressure point method. Hold the leash either up and back, or across the front of your calf (for very active, squiggly dogs such as puppies) or just straight up and back. At the same time, use the thumb and index finger of your other hand to squeeze at the rear pressure points located just above

Scoop the dog's rear into a sitting position.

Gently massage the dog's rear when he is in the Sit.

your dog's hips. You should not be trying to shove your dog into a Sit; rather, apply pressure on these points so he sits himself. As he begins to squat, say the word Sit.

If you have a dog with an extremely laid back character you can use one hand in front of his chest and the other on the pressure points.

If your dog is very muscular, chubby or big, it may be difficult to find the pressure points or they may be too far apart for your fingers. In this case, try putting the collar a bit higher on the neck, just under the chin, and gently pulling up while you also push down on the rump with your other hand (or use your foot for really big dogs).

The scoop method is generally good for sensitive dogs. Hold the leash in the same way as in the pressure point method, up and back, but you will use your other hand to tuck in the dog's rear. As the dog is going into the position, say Sit.

With the touch method you are simply applying the same pressure up and slightly back with the leash, but you are using the flat of your palm to apply pressure on the dog's rear.

DOWN

For this command, you are not teaching the dog how to lie down—he already knows how to do that. You are teaching him that when we say the word Down, he should lie down until he's told to do something else. The conventional way is to have the dog Sit first. Although this makes it a little easier for the dog because he is halfway there already, it is not teaching him the proper command. Sit and Down are separate commands and should not be linked in training.

There are several ways to place a dog in the Down position, depending on the size and character of the dog. You should choose the one that is best suited for you and your dog. Down should be easy for the dog to understand, so if it takes more than seven seconds for the dog to lie down, try another method. This is not about a struggle or fight, and you don't want the dog to panic or you to get frustrated. Teaching should be fast and easy for both of you.

With each method, you will say the word Down as the dog is already in the process of dropping down, not before or after.

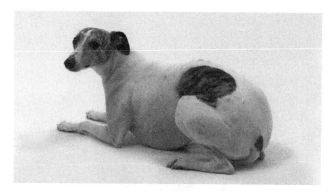

Prone down

Hip down

Side down

Steady pressure is applied on the points behind the dog's shoulder blades and on the leash held below his chin.

As the dog begins to drop, say the command word Down.

Once the dog is in the Down you can praise with your voice and gently massage between his shoulder blades.

With the same hand that is holding the leash, gently lift one of the dog's front paws up and out. As he begins to drop into the position, say the word Down.

There are three ways a dog can lie down. The first is a prone Down, where the dog is lying like a sphinx. The dog is most likely to break the command in this position because he is not relaxed into it. The second is a hip Down, where the dog is leaning on one hip. It usually means the dog is more relaxed and is less likely to get up from the position.

The third is a side Down, where the dog lies flopped on one side. While the dog is probably very relaxed in this position, sometimes dogs who flop over to the side when placed in a Down are beginning to play around too much.

The pressure point method used to teach Sit also works for Down, but this time use the thumb and index finger of one hand to gently squeeze at the pressure points located just behind your dog's shoulder blades. Be sure not to shove down—you are squeezing so the dog drops himself. At the same time, hold the leash just under the dog's chin with your other hand and apply pressure forward and down. Within three to five seconds the dog should be down. If it takes any longer it is a struggle and you should try another method.

The pressure and paw method is similar to the pressure point method, except you will gently take one front paw and lift it out at the same time as you are squeezing on the dog's pressure points.

Another way to help your dog into position is by holding the leash under the dog's chin, applying gentle pressure out and down towards the ground. At the same time apply pressure right above the crest of the dog's neck. As he drops into the position say the word Down. Release the pressure when he is in position, then praise calmly and gently rub near his shoulder blades.

If these methods don't work for you and your dog, stand straight up and lift the leash so it is taut. Step on the leash about six or seven inches from the dog's collar

For some dogs, applying pressure to the points just behind his shoulders at the same time as you step down on the taut leash makes for an easier drop into the Down.

Your hand should be spread as far across the dog's neck as possible to give you the best control.

and apply constant pressure downward until the dog is in the Down position. You may want to try applying pressure to his points just behind his shoulders at the same time as you step down on the taut leash.

For a dog who has a tendency to nip or is more sensitive to being touched on his shoulders, try putting two leashes on the dog. Tie one to a post, a couch leg or a tree, and with the other leash use the method described above. This will lessen the likelihood that you will struggle to keep the dog in one place.

For yet another method, hold the leash under the dog's chin and use the space between your thumb and index finger to apply pressure behind the dog's neck at the base of his head, gently pushing him towards the ground. You may also want to try lifting the dog's front paw that is nearest to you.

You can also mix methods. If you choose to step on the leash, for example, and the dog is struggling with you, try applying pressure at the points described above. Another example of mixing methods is that you may choose to start with the pressure points, but if your dog starts to nip at your hands when you pull the leash down and forward (as a puppy is likely to do), try stepping on the leash.

With all of these methods you should avoid touching the dog to praise him until he is all the way down.

THE WHOLE CONCEPT OF SIT AND DOWN

Once you have found the method that is most effective for placing your dog in a Sit or Down, it is time to teach him the whole concept of these commands: that he has to stay put until you say otherwise. If you do this with the Sit, by the time you get to the Down your dog will already understand that when you place him somewhere it means to stay there.

Place the dog in a Sit, and as he is going into the position say Sit. Drop the leash in front of him but keep one hand on his rear end and the other on his

This Rhodesian Ridgeback is being encouraged to stay in the Sit.

Fabian will drop the leash in front of the dog so he knows he is loose. He will stand straight up but will not step away yet.

When you walk away, try to act as natural as possible.

chest. Most adult dogs are already in the habit of sitting and getting right back up. Keep your hands on the dog for the first five to 10 placements to decrease your frustration at having to constantly replace the dog and to start building a new habit in the dog of sitting for longer than a few seconds. After a few moments, release the dog using your chosen release word.

After five to 10 placements with your hands on the dog's rear and chest, drop the leash in front of him. Make it obvious so that you're sure he knows you are not holding the leash. Stand up and then bend down again to praise the dog. If he gets up from the position, do not say anything. Do not verbally correct him and don't say the command again. Let the dog figure out the situation for himself. In real life, you don't want to have to constantly repeat commands, so don't do so in foundation training.

If he gets up, calmly bend down and replace him into the position using your chosen method. Don't get upset when you have to replace your dog. Remember, the only way for him to learn is by making mistakes. If anything, see each opportunity to replace him as a chance to make the concept of Sit clearer to him.

Wait a few seconds. Now stand up, pick up the leash, release him and walk a few steps with the dog. Place your hand gently under his tummy when you stop to keep him standing. (We don't want him to sit on his own yet—we want him to learn the word, then the habit.)

Place your hand gently under the dog's tummy to support him.

Praise him for stopping with you, then say Sit and drop the leash and praise. After a few moments, release the dog.

If you have to replace the dog more than three times when you are just standing up straight, then stay with him for a few more placements.

When you can do this about five times without replacing the dog, you can move on to teaching the full concept of the command. That is, he should be able to remain in position even if you walk away. When you walk away, don't face your dog. Try not to make direct eye contact. Instead, watch him out of the corner of your eye; otherwise you might give mixed signals and unintentionally call him with your eyes. You don't want him to be thinking about following you, especially if the dog is attached to you or if you have glared at the dog to punish him in the past. In real life, if you walk away from your dog you won't stand and stare straight at him, so don't teach it that way.

Your dog will almost definitely get up. When he does, just take him back to the same spot and replace him into the Sit, but do not say Sit again. It is his job to remember the command. You don't want a dog who you have to constantly remind in real life, so don't let him develop that habit in the foundation training.

Signs that your dog is considering getting up are bobbing his head down or looking side to side. Don't dive in to replace or correct. Give it a moment and let the dog get up if he wants to. This is the only way you will know what your dog has learned. When he starts to test the situation it is a good sign that he is beginning to think about the concept of the command.

If he lifts his rear off the ground and replaces it don't go in to replace or correct him, because you want to praise him for making the right choice. Wait a moment to see what choice he makes.

When you can put him in a Sit or Down position three times without a replacement, you know he is starting to understand the full concept of the command. At this point he knows what you expect and therefore must now also learn the consequences of not following the rules.

CORRECTIONS

You should not be the cause of any corrections from your dog's point of view. Don't use your voice to correct or the dog will lose focus on the command because he will be thinking more about your voice. We want him to understand that getting up from a command before being released causes a negative consequence.

When giving a correction think about how many times you want to correct your dog. Presumably, as few as possible. So do it effectively and you won't have to keep doing it again and again. On average, three to four corrections is too many for any one behavior. If you give three corrections and they aren't having an effect, try a different correction.

Place your dog on a Sit or Down. If he stands up but stays in the same place, just calmly walk over to him. Try not to make eye contact with him. If you are correcting for a Sit, snap the leash back and to the side; for a Down snap the leash down and to the side. When he is back in the position you placed him in, walk away. About five or 10 seconds later, come back, praise him and walk away again. Then come back, praise him and release him.

You should be able to leave your dog on a Down while you have a conversation with someone. If he gets up but stays in the same place, walk over to him without making eye contact or saying anything.

You may choose to replace the dog into the position or to correct him, depending on the stage of the teaching process and the situation.

Once the dog is in position again, walk away and go back to what you were doing.

After a few moments walk back to the dog and offer praise for being in the correct position.

If your dog breaks a command and moves away from the spot where he was replaced, calmly walk over to him, take his leash, and guide him back to the spot where he was originally placed.

When the dog is back in the original spot where he was placed, snap the leash down to the ground.

Leave the dog and go back to what you were doing.

After a few moments come back to the dog and praise him while he is in the position he was placed in.

Remember, do not correct your dog if he goes from a Sit into a Down when you walk away from him. Correct only if he stands up from a Sit or goes from a Down to a Sit or stands up. And if the dog gets up because something truly scared him, just replace him without a correction.

If he stands up and moves from the spot, calmly walk over to the leash and snap it forward until you get back to the spot where you originally placed him. Be sure not to make eye contact or to verbally reprimand the dog.

Snap the leash back and to the side for a Sit and down and to the side for a Down. For some dogs and owners it is better to give a correction by lifting the leash and stepping on it close to the dog's collar when it is taut. In this way you keep your hands clear when making a correction.

When the dog is back in the position you originally placed him in, walk away. About five to 10 seconds later, come back, praise him and walk away again. Then come back, praise him and release him.

Your goal in foundation training is to put the dog in a Sit or Down and walk away, with no need to correct or replace the dog. In foundation training you should expect to be able to leave your dog for 15 to 20 seconds if he's a puppy and at least a minute for a dog six months or older. Remember, it is all right for him to lie down and get comfortable. Don't push the dog to see how long you can make him stay—this is about teaching now, not pushing the limits.

At this stage you can use treats as a bonus reward. Just be sure to give the treat when the dog is on the command, not when you release him from it, so he associates the bonus with the command. It is more valuable to use treats when the dog already understands what you are trying to teach him. Otherwise the food might divert him from the learning process. You want him to follow commands because it is what you expect of him and because he learns that obeying commands is enjoyable in itself, not because he is submitting to receive the food. Using food to teach is not wrong, it just makes it harder in the long run for the dog to learn.

LIFESTYLE TRAINING FOR SIT AND DOWN

Once your dog understands the concept of Sit, Down should only take a short time to teach and should then be immediately applied to real life. For the first few days of lifestyle training, make sure he understands the commands in all sorts of new situations by placing and replacing him. There should be no corrections in lifestyle training yet.

Your dog must clearly understand what is expected before he receives a correction. It would be unfair to correct an animal, or a person for that matter, until he clearly understands the rules.

Once you can place your dog, without replacements, at least three times for each command, he is ready for a correction for breaking the command. A correction teaches that breaking the command is no longer an option.

COME

This is certainly the most important command you can teach your dog, as it could save his life one day. We teach Come to have two purposes: It means Come With Me, as in walking without pulling on the leash; and Come To Me, as in the traditional recall where the dog comes to you from a distance. You want the dog to understand the best place to be is at your side. Not coming to you could cause a negative, and in real life this negative could be dangerous.

Be sure to be consistent in the way in which you ask your dog to walk with you. Before you begin, choose which side you would like your dog to walk on and stick with it. It is dangerous to have a dog who criss-crosses in front of your path to switch sides.

You should avoid using this command if you are calling your dog to do something he doesn't enjoy very much. For example, if you are going to give your dog a bath it might be better to go get him rather than to call him to come to you. We want him to associate coming to you and with you with positive experiences.

Don't use this command (or any command, for that matter) off leash—even indoors—until you are

A dog who clearly understands the concept of the Come command knows he must pay attention even when passing other dogs.

Fabian is letting the dog make the choice of going away from him by slackening the leash.

Whichever way the dog chooses to go, Fabian will turn sharply in the opposite direction. This way, the dog will get an automatic leash correction.

For most dogs it takes only a few corrections before they realize it is more pleasurable to keep an eye on which way the person at the other end of the leash is going than to blaze their own trail at the end of a tight leash.

confident that he is as close to perfect on leash as possible. If you call your off-leash dog to Come and he doesn't respond, he has learned that he doesn't always have to obey Come. If you are diligent about setting up a lot of distractions and calling him when he is on leash, you will be setting a very strong foundation for off-leash control.

If you have a dog who has already spent some time being allowed to pull on the leash, don't be surprised if you have to spend a bit more time building a new habit of not pulling to override the old habit of pulling. It is very easy to teach a puppy who has no bad habits yet, because you have the opportunity to teach him right from the very beginning.

For an adult dog or puppy who has already developed a habit of pulling you, you first must create a fracture for this training to work. Go back to Chapter Four and create the fracture before you go any further.

You should also consider changing equipment. If the dog is pulling with a buckle collar, it means he is probably immune to a correction with this collar. If the dog is already pulling on a slip collar, you might want to try a baby or medium pinch collar. The next chapter discusses collars and leashes and how to use them in training.

Let's start with Come With Me. Begin by calling the dog's name and saying Come. Walk off as you say it. If your dog goes ahead of you, let him go to the

Snap the leash straight back as you make a left turn.

Turn directly into the dog. He should be paying attention and get out of your way—you should not get out of his.

Your turn should head you straight back in the opposite direction.

The dog will now be watching you because he is learning he must in order to stay out of your way.

end of the leash, then run the opposite way. This will cause an automatic correction. As soon as he starts going your way, praise him. It is his job to pay attention and walk with you. If he chooses to go in a direction other than the one you have chosen, let him. But he will learn that the consequence for him is that he might lose track of you. Repeat this process until you see him start to pay atention to you. By this we mean he is walking close to you; he doesn't have to be glued to your side.

Now start making left turns. Snap the leash straight back as you turn sharply to the left. Do not move out of the dog's way, and do not give him any indication that you are turning. You want the dog to move out of your way, not vice versa. This will teach him to pay closer attention to you because he never knows when you will turn. You'll start to see him closely watching you and almost hop out of your way when you turn.

After a day or two, when he is responding to your movements, you can say the dog's name as you change direction with the word Come. Be sure to change direction suddenly. He must feel the need to be more focused on you than on anything else, and you encourage this by keeping him guessing as to which way you are going. As soon as he changes directions with you, praise. Try to lose him; it is his job to find you, and your job to praise him for doing so.

The Come To Me part of the command is very easy once you have taught your dog to walk on the leash without pulling. You will need a longer leash; approximately 10 feet is good.

When the dog is distracted, say his name and Come. If he turns to look at you, praise and encourage him to move to you. If he doesn't turn to look at you snap the leash and then praise when he turns to you. Praise and encourage as he moves in to you. If he gets distracted along the way, do not say the command or his name again. It is his job to remember that he is on a command. Snap the leash again and praise when he is redirected to you.

It is most effective to use this command in foundation training when the dog is not focused on training. Call him when he is interested in his own doggy business. This is most likely the way you will use the command in real life, so use it that way when you're training, too. It would be silly to place your dog on a Sit, step to the end of a leash and call him from there because you would never need to do this in real life.

PROOFING

Proofing is the process of setting up situations to make sure your dog understands the commands you've taught him. When your dog is on a Sit or Down, come back to your dog, pick up the leash, praise him, drop the leash and walk away again. He has to really think in this situation. But if he is to clearly understand the command, this is a fair situation to put him in. Even though you came back to him, you did not release him or command him to Come.

This miniature Poodle is avoiding eye contact with the source of a distraction. He knows that Sit means do so no matter what is going on. Notice that the leash is slack—the dog must make the choice to stay in the Sit.

If he makes all the right choices, try coming back to him, picking up the leash and taking a small step away with the leash in your hand (be careful to keep the leash slack). Again, even though you stepped away you didn't release him or say Come, so he is still on command.

You should also tempt the dog with things that will distract him from you and your command, such as noise, children and other dogs. You should definitely use real-life situations to train, but sometimes, especially when you're dealing with specific behavior problems, you must set up situations in order to speed up the training process.

This is often misinterpreted as teasing a dog, but what this actually does is make it easier for the dog to understand that the command means the same thing no matter what else is going on. Confused dogs are forced to decide when an owner really means it and when they can slack off on a command. For example, if

This owner takes his dog with him to his pet supply store. This dog must obey commands under some of the most difficult distractions—strange dogs and enticing treats are all around him. He clearly understands that Down means Down no matter what is going on.

you say Down and a child walks by with a hot-dog, does your dog still have to stay down? When your hands are full of groceries and you say Sit, do you mean it? If your dog is not sure, you're asking for trouble.

When he is responding to his name and comes without you having to snap the leash, start to take him to new places and use the command. Allow him to be distracted the same way you did at home. After a few times practicing in each new place, he will be more focused on you because it is more pleasurable than being distracted. He will learn that near you is the safest and most pleasurable place to be.

TRAINING TOOLS

The wide variety of collars, leashes and other tools available to train your dog is large and sometimes confusing. Don't let any salesperson or trainer insist you use any particular piece of equipment—different training tools suit different types of dogs.

COLLARS

Some trainers promote the use of one type of collar , usually a slip collar, to train all types of dogs. This is unrealistic; there is no one collar that is appropriate for all dogs. While a flat leather collar is preferable, training equipment must be matched to the temperament of the individual dog and owner.

Use a flat collar made of nylon or leather for a puppy's first collar. The wider the collar, the less severe correction it will give. If used effectively,

this can be the type of collar a dog uses for the remainder of his life. However, if not used properly this collar can quickly become ineffective.

At a young age many puppies are allowed, often even encouraged, to pull on a buckle collar. By the time the dog is an adolescent, he is usually immune to any sort of correction with a buckle collar. In this case the owner must now use a different collar, usually a slip or pinch, in order to make an effective correction.

There are also certain situations, such as adopting an older dog, in which the dog's history of training warrants a different training tool. His previous owners may have worn out the usefulness of the buckle collar. They allowed control to slip away with that tool, so

Top from left to right: medium pinch, baby pinch and flat buckle collar. Bottom from left to right: Halti collar, chain slip collar and nylon slip collar.

the new owner might have to try a different collar in order to make a difference. There are also situations where a dog, even an adolescent, has such a strong character that a buckle collar will not be effective.

Of course, the match of dog to owner also plays a big part in how effective a specific tool will be. If an owner with a very soft character is matched with a dog with a very strong character, the choice of tools might be very different than if the roles were reversed.

When the appropriate tool is found, the collar should enable the owner to make a quick and effective correction.

The choke or slip collar is referred to by many people as the training collar. This label makes it seem as though this is the only collar a dog should be trained with, which is absolutely not true. It should not be considered standard training equipment because it is not needed or even appropriate for every dog or every owner.

This collar will not help you magically get control of your dog. In fact, the average person today uses this collar incorrectly, so in that sense it can be cruel. The slip collar is not meant to cause constant discomfort or pain to your dog, but only to cause a brief negative. Furthermore, you don't want any negative to become a lifestyle for your dog. A correction should be used as briefly as possible to aid in the learning process, but the majority of your dog's life should be positive.

Imagine Fabian's arm is the dog's neck. If you choose to walk your dog on your left, this is how the slip collar should be placed.

There are chain and nylon slip collars. Try the nylon one first. With chain collars the dog hears the correction and is less likely to be focused on thinking about the problem at hand. When the dog is being corrected, it is better if he associates the correction with the problem, not the problem with the noise.

While a nylon slip collar is preferable, if you choose a chain slip collar, you might want to steer clear of the ones made of small circular rings. They tend to rip off hair and discolor the throat hairs. The chain collars made of oblong rings, or the Woodhouse-type collars, are preferable.

This is how the collar will tighten.

It is imperative that after a quick snap to tighten the collar, you allow it to slacken just as quickly. If you put the collar on correctly, it will slacken as soon as you ease up.

To be fit properly, this collar should have only two inches of slack when placed on the dog's neck. It should be placed in such a way that when the leash is slack, so is the collar.

The slip collar should never be left on your dog when he is unsupervised or in his crate, because a ring could get caught on something and choke the dog.

You might also consider the humane choker or half choke. When properly fitted, this collar can only get so snug. It also might be considered a bit safer than a flat collar in that it cannot slip over the dog's head if he backs up while on leash.

The Halti or Gentle Leader collars resemble halters used to lead horses by their head. They are sometimes mistaken for muzzles, but they actually do not restrict the dog's ability to open his mouth. They can be very valuable for someone who doesn't feel they are physically strong enough to control their dog.

True harnesses give very little control. They allow the pressure of the dog's pulling to be distributed across his body. These are used for tracking and sledding dogs to make pulling easier and more comfortable. So if you have a dog who already pulls, this tool will probably be ineffective. But if used on a very young puppy, it can be much like a buckle collar. If your veterinarian has recommended that you use a harness due to a medical condition, such as a tracheal

If the dog is walking to your left, this would be the wrong way to put on a slip collar.

Notice that even when Fabian is completely slackening the end of the collar, it does not loosen up around his arm. This collar was put on wrong.

problem, ask him if he is comfortable with you using a Halti or Gentle Leader instead.

A pinch collar works by causing a pinching sensation when tightened. In itself this collar is not cruel, but how it is used can be. If the dog is immune to a flat or slip collar, this may be an option. However, as with any training tool, a pinch collar can also become ineffective if improperly used.

All training tools should be used so that they don't have to be used. This means if you choose to use a pinch collar, the corrections given with it should make such an impression on the dog that you won't have to keep giving corrections with the collar. You are using the collar to help explain to your dog that he shouldn't pull, for example, because doing so results in the negative feeling of the pinch collar tightening. Once he makes this association, he won't want to pull because he has learned that it only results in negatives, so you won't have to correct with the collar. You may even be able to go back to a simple buckle collar after the habit of walking politely on a leash has been established.

LEASHES

The choice of a leash depends on the size and strength of your dog and the terrain where he will be walked. Fabian's preference is a four- or six-foot leather leash because leather is generally softer on your hands than nylon. Four feet of leash is usually easier for a novice handler to work with because there isn't so much to get tangled up with. If you have a puppy, you may want to start off with a nylon leash until he understands that chewing on the leash is inappropriate.

A long leash (at least 10 feet) is a great training aid to establish control from a distance. You can buy one from a pet supply store, or buy clothesline and a stainless steel clip from a hardware store and make your own.

Leashes that extend and retract should not be used when doing foundation training with your dog. You won't be able to teach him how to walk on the leash without pulling if the leash is always taut, as it is with

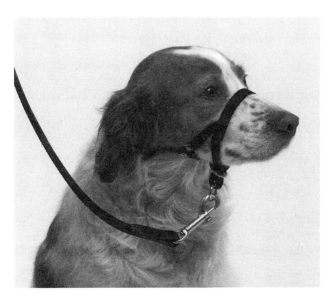

If introduced properly, the Halti collar can be an effective training tool.

this sort of leash, and if his distance from you is always changing. If you use this leash on a trained dog, be careful not to grab the line, as you can get a rope burn.

Remember that no matter how well trained your dog is, he must be on a leash outside. Aside from being illegal in most areas, it isn't fair to him or to people he may come into contact with if he isn't on a leash.

CORRECTION TOOLS

Used properly, a throw can, chain and small bean bag can be very effective training aides to solve a lot of unwanted behaviors. They should be used to create a correction that the dog will not associate with you, but only with the behavior he was performing.

A throw can is a homemade training tool. Empty the soda from an aluminum soda can, and fill it with a few pennies or paper clips. Then cover the top of the can with tape. This tool is used to cause a negative consequence when your dog is behaving in ways you find inappropriate.

The can should be tossed at your dog's rear end and must make contact with him. It is not meant to cause pain—the can, even with its new contents, is very light—but rather to startle your dog.

Some people suggest using the throw can to simply make a rattling noise to startle the dog. That might work on a dog with a softer character, but it won't work with every dog because the sound will only surprise and startle for a limited time. Repeating the noise as a correction will only get the dog accustomed

Some correction tools: a throw chain and throw can.

to the sound, until he realizes there is no real consequence to hearing it. That is why the throw can should actually make contact with the dog.

Two other tools that should be used in the same way are the bean bag and the throw chain. It's easy to make a small bean bag yourself from a scrap of cloth and a handful of beans. Keep the size appropriate for your dog, and in any case, make the bean bag small so it doesn't hurt.

A throw chain is another correction tool. This is a small, light chain that you will also throw at the dog's rump. You can buy a specially made one or use a small chain slip collar designed for a smaller dog. Be careful using this, as you do not want to hurt your dog.

When using one of these tools, as with any correction, you must be as unemotional as possible. This means no verbal or eye contact with the dog, to ensure that the dog doesn't associate the correction with you.

After you toss the object, the dog will look around to see what happened. When he looks to you, your job is to encourage him to continue to focus on you. Remember, you are all about being positive to your dog.

YOUR HANDS

Your hands are wonderful training tools, but they should have a limited purpose. They should be used to mold your dog into positions, to praise with touch and to occasionally offer treats. They should never be used to hit your dog.

STARTING YOUR PUPPY OUT RIGHT

So far the concepts we've been discussing apply to all dogs, young and old. But the truth is, when most people bring a new dog into their home, it's a puppy. Puppies have special needs and require special understanding. They also present special opportunities to avoid the bad habits that make too many dogs poor companions, and to build a bond of trust and respect that will last a lifetime.

Your first three steps as a new puppy owner should be to clearly define what it is you will expect from your puppy as an adult dog, to learn how to clearly express this to him and to have confidence that your young puppy is mentally capable of understanding your fair and humane expectations.

The foundation training explained in Chapter Five also applies to your puppy. Just remember to be extremely gentle with corrections and to use them very sparingly. But there are other things to do first.

CHOOSE THE RULES

Before you even consider teaching your puppy Sit or Down, you should sit down, along with everyone else in your household, and write down what each of you will expect from your new friend when he is an adult. Is he to be allowed on the furniture? Is he expected to respond to commands the first time they are given? Is he allowed to jump on people? Only by having a clear set of rules will you be able to clearly convey to your puppy what you expect of him.

Be sure the rules you want your puppy to live by are fair. For example, it would be unfair to say you want a dog who only needs to eliminate once or twice a day.

It is important when you're setting the rules to think about what you want the puppy to do as an adult, because that is what he will be for the majority of his life. Too many people allow their puppies to behave in ways that are perceived as cute for a puppy (for example, tugging on the fringe of a robe or slipper or jumping all over people to say hello). But do you want an adult dog who greets people by jumping all over them? It is unfair to allow a puppy to behave in certain ways that will be considered inappropriate when he grows up. It would be comparable to allowing a child to pinch or slap people until the age of 12, and then all of a sudden expecting him to understand that physical violence is inappropriate.

Don't think that when your puppy becomes an adult he will outgrow certain behaviors. In fact, the opposite is true. Behaviors that are allowed to develop in puppyhood, such as jumping on people, eliminating in the house and chewing on hands and furniture, will become deep-rooted habits by the time your dog reaches maturity. If you want an adult dog who will behave in a certain way, you must expect that same behavior from your puppy. Explaining the rules to your puppy from the first day he arrives in your home is the most humane thing you can do for him.

Nobody who gets a puppy ever thinks they'll be giving their new friend up to a shelter. But that is just where so many potentially wonderful dogs are left, due in great part to the fact that the rules of the human world were not clearly explained to them during puppyhood. Enjoy your puppy and some of his puppy antics, but do so as a responsible owner. Don't allow him to do things that will be detrimental to him and others later on.

FOLLOW THE RULES

The boundaries and rules you set down for your new puppy must be rigidly followed by everyone in the household for the first eight or nine months of his life. This does not mean you can't enjoy your dog's puppyhood or that he must live as though he were in the Marine Corps. But by sticking closely to the rules through your dog's adolescence, you will be establishing behaviors that will become lifetime habits. If you show your puppy that he must sit to greet people by placing him in a Sit position and helping him by gently massaging his rear to encourage staying in that position, there will quickly come a point when you won't even have to command your puppy to Sit—he will do so automatically when someone comes to say hello to him, simply out of habit. By sticking rigidly to the rules, you will be making it easier for your puppy to clearly understand how to behave as an adult in order to fit into your lifestyle.

The entire household must help the puppy by sticking to the same rules. If they don't, it will be very confusing to the dog. For example, if one person doesn't want the puppy on any furniture but another allows him on the couch when nobody else is around, the puppy will not be clear as to what the rules are regarding the furniture.

For many years the general rule in dog training was to wait until a puppy reached the age of about six months before beginning training. This would be like waiting to teach a child how to behave in society until he is 12 years old. Puppies are learning during every moment of their lives. You can have a lot of control over what they learn and can play a great part in determining the behavior of your dog as an adult. So begin training from the first day you bring your puppy home. His brain is like a sponge, ready to absorb all of the information you provide.

Avoid creating problems in your dog's puppyhood that you will have to deal with when he is an adult. Don't offer toys that resemble household objects you don't want your puppy to chew. Don't avoid grooming a puppy that you know will need a lot of grooming as an adult. Puppyhood lasts a very short time, but you will want your well-educated adult dog to be with you for a long time.

BEFORE YOU BRING YOUR PUPPY HOME

You will help your puppy make a smooth transition into your home if you spend time preparing for his arrival. A well-planned introduction into your home will be less stressful for you both. To begin, you should acquire some basic supplies.

Gate A puppy or baby gate is helpful for supervised play times. Blocking off areas allows the puppy to stay confined while you keep your eyes on him. It keeps him from roaming out of your sight and leaving accidents or getting into other trouble.

Leash and Collar A nylon leash is recommended for puppies. This type of leash is cheaper and therefore

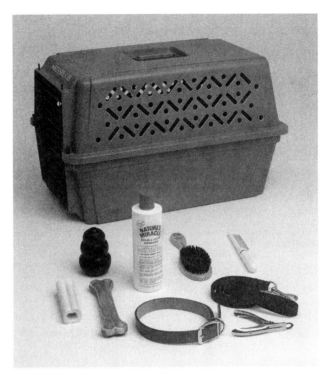

These are some of the basics every puppy requires.

more dispensable than other types, in case your puppy gets in a few chews before you notice. For the collar, a flat nylon or leather buckle collar is appropriate for puppies. The greater the width of the flat collar, the easier it is on the puppy's neck. (For more on collars and leashes, see Chapter Six.)

Toys Be sure the toys you choose are safe. In other words, if they have small parts or are squeaky toys, the puppy should only play with them when someone is supervising him. White sterilized bones and Nyla

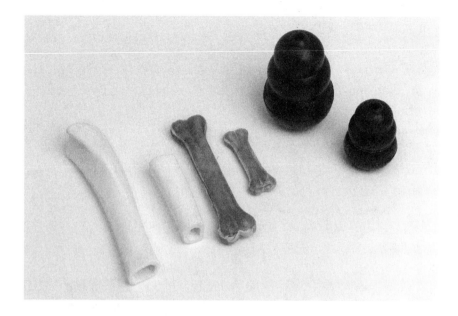

Your puppy needs appropriate toys to satisfy his need to chew.

bones are safe as long as they are the appropriate size for your puppy. If they are too small, there is a danger he could choke on them. Use common sense, and talk to your veterinarian about any specific questions.

Chew Deterrents You might want to purchase a chewing deterrent product such as Bitter Apple, but again, if you are supervising your puppy he won't have the opportunity to become a destructive chewer. Your puppy does need things to chew on, so make sure you give him suitable toys to redirect his chewing.

Food and Water Bowls Stainless steel bowls are recommended. These are durable and easy to clean and disinfect.

Food Try to get a one-week supply of the food the puppy is currently eating. This can be mixed with a new food, if you decide to switch. Over about a three-day period, gradually feed less of the old food and more of the new food. Try not to make an abrupt change in food—this can sometimes cause an upset stomach and loose stools.

Grooming Supplies These will depend on the type of coat your puppy has. But most dogs will do well with a soft brush, dog shampoo (do not use human shampoo on dogs), nail clippers, a toothbrush and ear cleaning swabs.

Crate Any time you can't keep an eye on your puppy he should be safely confined. Just like a child's crib or playpen, your puppy will be safe and happy in his crate if you teach him to be. There are a wide variety of crate sizes and styles on the market. The two

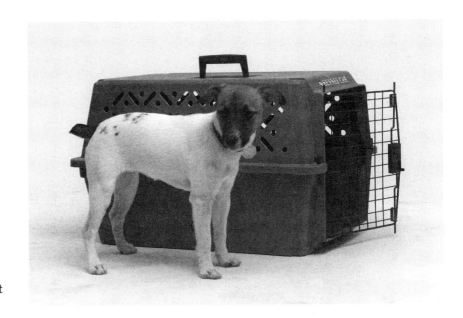

This crate is just big enough for this puppy, but he will probably outgrow it in a very short time.

most common choices are metal and plastic. For most puppies the plastic crate is preferred, as it is a bit safer; some puppies can get their paws caught in the small openings of the wire crates.

The most important factor in choosing a crate is the size. It should be just big enough for the puppy to stand up, turn around and lie down. Do not buy a crate that will fit the puppy when he grows to his adult size. If you do, it is very likely the puppy will use one part of the crate as a bedroom and the other as a bathroom. While a puppy-size crate means you might have to buy another crate as the dog grows, this expense will be offset by the savings in cleaning fluids used for a dog who eliminates in the house because he learned it was okay to do so in his crate. If you must

buy a larger crate, block off a section of it so it is properly sized for your pup.

AN OUNCE OF PREVENTION

Just as you would take precautions when bringing home a new human baby, you must do so when bringing home a canine baby. Taking a few preventive measures can greatly decrease the possibility of a tragedy. Even if you are diligent about supervising your puppy, there will inevitably come a time when he will somehow find his way out of your sight, which is why your home should be puppy-proofed.

Walk through your house, room by room, and look for things at floor level or puppy eye level that might get a young animal into trouble. Use your imagination—your puppy will use his!

Kitchen Your puppy can use his paws or muzzle to pry open a cabinet, so install locks or otherwise securely shut the cabinets to keep your puppy away from harmful cleaning fluids. Also, invest in a garbage can that locks shut; there are many dangerous objects, such as bones, glass and metal, in your garbage can.

Bathroom Make sure all cosmetics, toiletries and especially razors are kept out of reach. Pay special attention to drugs such as aspirin. You should secure low cabinets just as you would for a child. Don't leave rugs or towels in the puppy's reach—he is likely to shred them.

Bedroom Beware of jewelry and other sharp metal objects that might be within reach. Also, be careful about what kinds of objects you leave on your night stand, such as prescription medicines.

Living Room Electrical cords and toxic houseplants are the two biggest hazards in most living rooms. If your household has children and they use the living room as a play room, make sure all the kids' toys are out of the puppy's reach. Also, secure the windows to ensure your puppy doesn't fall out.

Garage or Basement This is often the most dangerous area for a dog. Be careful that poisons for insects and rodents, wires, car oils, anti-freeze and fertilizers are out of reach. Watch for spills on the floor.

Yard The biggest dangers in the yard are usually toxic plants and insecticides. Even something spread on the grass can end up in your puppy's system when he licks his paws after a romp in the yard.

PUPPY COMES HOME

It is usually advisable to bring a new dog home on a day when you do not have to go to work and to schedule the pickup for early in the day. This way you have all day to spend time with him. You may want to arrange for someone to come with you so they can drive while you pay attention to the puppy. Young pups get carsick very easily, so bring paper towels, some type of all-purpose cleaner and plastic bags with you just in case.

When you arrive home, immediately put the puppy down in an appropriate area to relieve himself. If he does, praise him.

The puppy should be on a leash so you can control him. When you bring him into your home, try to keep things as calm as possible. Of course everyone will want to say hello to the new baby, but be fair and let one or two people at a time calmly say hello. Place the puppy in an area where there is no rug, so if he has an accident it will be easier to clean up. Remember that puppies are easily excited and simply do not have the bladder and bowel control of adult dogs. Watch for signs that he needs to relieve himself, such as circling and sniffing. If you notice these signs, immediately take the pup outside or to an area where you've put down paper.

The moment your puppy enters your home, the rules you and your family have set up for him should be followed—forming good habits begins from day one. When your child goes to school, the teacher sets down classroom rules on the first day. You are your puppy's teacher. Help him to quickly adjust to his new home by clearly defining the rules.

For example, if you are watching the puppy investigate his new surroundings and he starts to chew on an inappropriate object, make a loud noise, such as dropping a book. Do not use your voice. As soon as the puppy stops what he is doing you will be there to use your voice to praise him. You should also offer him an acceptable chew toy, immediately redirecting his natural behavior from an inappropriate object to an appropriate one.

As the puppy gets more comfortable in his new surroundings, he will begin to test his status. He will probably want to try to climb on you and nip you. Again, if these behaviors are not acceptable to you they should be stopped immediately. As soon as he jumps on you, help him into a Sit. You may also make him think he just pushed your fast forward button—immediately walk forward very quickly, pushing the puppy back. As soon as all four of his paws are on the ground, praise him. This will show him that the pleasure of your attention is enjoyed only when he's on the ground.

As for mouthing and nipping, most people think it is normal for a puppy to teethe. It is, but he should never teethe on human hands. If it is all right to chew on a hand as a puppy, why shouldn't he think it is

acceptable as an adult dog? Solve this problem before it gets out of hand. When the pup goes to nip, do not take your hand away. Your goal is to teach him to choose to take his mouth off your hand. Place your thumb on his tongue and push down. As soon as he releases your hand, praise and pet him. If a smaller child is playing with the puppy, you as an adult can use a light object, such as a small bean bag, to throw at his rear end. When the pup stops, immediately praise him. And *never* let a child administer a correction. If you are careful to supervise all interactions between your puppy and any children he meets, you will be able to quickly show both how to interact with each other.

Some puppies adjust to their new home more quickly than others. If your puppy is unsure of his surroundings, remember he is used to sleeping with his litter mates. New pups should be sleeping in a crate (more on crate training in a moment). Playing soft music near the puppy's sleeping quarters might make things a little easier for him. You can keep the puppy's crate near your bed for a few nights. Also, you should keep some clothing that's easy to slip on so you can take him out in the middle of the night.

If the puppy won't stop crying at night, and you are as sure as you can be that he doesn't have to relieve himself, after about five or 10 minutes, try tossing a throw can at the crate without saying a word. When the puppy is quiet for at least five minutes, and only then, can you take him out of his crate to spend time with him. If you let your puppy out whenever he cries, he will learn that all he has to do is cry to get out whenever he wants. This is a bad habit you should avoid from the very beginning.

You can get your puppy used to relaxing in his crate by periodically putting him in it during the day and using the throw can if he cries. As he begins to settle down and regard the crate as his den, he will be less likely to cry at night.

As soon as you wake up, take the puppy out to relieve himself. If you can put off doing anything for yourself, such as making coffee, do so. You will be avoiding a big mess to clean up.

CRATE TRAINING

A crate or kennel is one of the most valuable tools any puppy or dog owner can acquire. It can be used to aid in-house training, preventing destructive behavior, safe car and plane travel, conditioning the dog to periods of separation from humans and protecting your dog from hurting himself in a number of ways, including chewing electrical cords and eating toxic substances.

One of the few things the crate should never be used for is to punish your dog. If you do this, he will associate the crate with punishment and may begin whimpering or barking when placed in his crate. The use of the crate should not be abused; don't leave your dog in there for hours on end, and don't allow anyone to tease your dog when he is in his crate—or out of it, for that matter.

If you use the crate properly, your puppy will see it as a safe, warm place, much like a bedroom. When you can't spend time with him, your puppy can do just about everything you'd want him to do in his crate: sleep, eat and play.

If you are getting your puppy from a reputable breeder, ask them if you can bring the crate over a few days before you actually pick up your puppy. This way, the puppy can get used to it. This may help to alleviate some of the puppy's stress when he enters a new environment. You might also bring something with your scent on it and put it in the crate.

Your puppy's first experiences with the crate should be as pleasurable as possible. You have to teach him that there is nothing to be afraid of when he's in the crate. While it is true that dogs were originally den animals, domesticated dogs are far removed from that natural behavior, and the denning instinct may be deeply buried in your puppy.

Don't assume that you can just put your puppy in a crate, walk away and he will be fine. Your puppy might panic. (Not every puppy will panic but you never know which ones will, so it's best to simply head it off before it has a chance to happen.) You cannot walk away from a panicky puppy in a crate, thinking he will eventually tire himself out and fall asleep. This is unrealistic and unfair. You might also end up with a puppy who associates his crate with fear and panic.

Introduce your puppy to his crate immediately after he has eliminated outside or on paper. Don't begin crate training when he is in a rambunctious mood or when a lot of activity is going on, either. Once you have established the crate as a safe place where the puppy goes to relax, you can put him in at just about any time (except when he needs to eliminate). But to start, wait until he is calm.

When first placing the puppy in the crate, don't attempt to drag him into it or even to entice him in with a toy or food. If you do so, you will be letting him decide if he wants to go in. Instead, gently lift him and place him in the crate. Allow the door to stay open, but keep your hand in front of the puppy's chest so he can't step out. Before he even has a chance to panic, praise him. If he panics, then you know he is a little more submissive in closed environments. So keep the door open for now but don't let him walk out.

After a few moments in the crate, let him walk out, but don't pay too much attention to him. You are teaching him that being in the crate is pleasurable and being out of it is not as much fun because he doesn't get your attention. Repeat this a few times, then close the door for about eight to 10 seconds. Slowly extend the time you keep the puppy in the crate with the door closed.

At this stage, you may want to offer a small treat every once in a while. If the puppy shows some displeasure with being in his crate, do not talk to him or show any sign that you feel sorry for him—this will only reinforce this behavior. Instead, praise the puppy in the moments that he is calm. Right from the beginning you want to create an atmosphere where going into the crate means relaxing.

If you set a solid foundation in crate training, that is, if you are fair in teaching him how safe he is in the crate, your puppy will not panic. That doesn't mean he might not cry, but he won't panic. If he does cry, let him do so for five or 10 minutes and then use the throw can. Toss it at the crate without making a sound yourself. You should only have to do this two or three times before your puppy learns that his crying creates the negative of the can hitting his crate.

Teaching your puppy to relax in his crate can help avoid separation anxiety. Many people spend an enormous amount of time with their puppies. This is understandable, but too much of anything is not always a good thing. Even if you spend a lot of time with your new puppy for the first two or three weeks, you may eventually find that your lifestyle doesn't allow you to keep up this kind of schedule. Your puppy, however, might have a difficult time dealing with a change in the level of attention. He may begin to exhibit signs of separation anxiety, such as excessive whining and barking, destructive behavior (including self-mutilation) and overall stress. If you frequently put your puppy in his crate for short periods of time, he will learn to feel comfortable without constant human company.

You should also feed your puppy in his crate. This way he will associate the crate with a good thing.

CHAPTER SEVEN

Gently place the puppy in the crate.

Use your hand on the puppy's chest to gently massage him and keep him in the crate.

After a few moments allow the puppy to step out of the crate.

Offer calm, gentle praise and then repeat this process.

Also, you don't want to start the pup off by just leaving food on the kitchen floor, because he is likely to wander around and get distracted. Your puppy should eat his whole meal in about 15 minutes, and it will be easier for him to do that if he's not distracted.

Feeding on a schedule will help with your puppy's house training. So will the crate. Most dogs are not comfortable soiling the area where they sleep, so by confining them to small sleeping quarters we are encouraging them to develop bladder and bowel control.

To begin, most puppies have an easier time if there are no objects in the crate. It seems that some puppies left with a blanket or towel to lie on are comfortable urinating on it and pushing it to the side. By setting a schedule where the puppy spends periods of time in the crate, you are building his control and avoiding accidents in the house that can quickly turn into soiling habits.

Many times people object to crates, saying "But I want my puppy to be free." Try not to view the crate as a jail for your dog; rather, it is like a playpen for a baby. All children go through a period of confinement and intense supervision during which they learn how to be safe for when they are eventually left unsupervised at an older age. If used properly, the crate will be the most effective tool in teaching your puppy how to be house trained and more, so he can have as much freedom in the house as you would like.

HOUSE TRAINING

House training means forming and establishing the habit of not eliminating in the home. Dogs are animals of habit, and most everything they learn becomes a habit for them. Your goal as a pet owner is to help your dog establish the habit of being clean in the house and eliminating outdoors.

Most dogs are fairly clean animals. Of course, some dogs deviate from the norm, especially puppies bought at pet stores where they are often expected to sleep and eliminate in the same quarters. But just as we were trained by our parents to use a bathroom, we can teach our dogs to use the outdoors as their bathroom.

Step one in puppy house training is a visit to the veterinarian to make sure your puppy is healthy. He must be clear of parasites and urinary infections. It would be unfair to expect a sick puppy to control himself. If there are any health problems, deal with them first.

Step two is to make sure you have a crate that's the right size for your pup, a leash and collar and an area outside for the dog to relieve himself.

Step three is to set up a food-and-water schedule. Do this with the help of your veterinarian. This schedule will help you to know exactly when your dog will need to eliminate. In general, puppies under four months old should be fed three times a day (morning, afternoon and early evening), and puppies four months to two years should be fed twice a day. Dogs two years and over can be fed once a day, but most people like to stick with two feedings to avoid any stress caused by hunger.

Water should be given at least three to four times a day and always when your dog comes in from exercising. You should check with your vet regarding the appropriate quantity for your puppy. In hot weather you can offer more water, but you will have to offer more opportunities for the dog to relieve himself. You may want to offer a few ice cubes in between waterings instead.

Food should only be left down for 15 minutes. If he picks at his food for an hour, you will have a hard time gauging when he will need to eliminate. If your puppy doesn't eat, he will at the next meal. The exception to this is if your vet orders otherwise for medical reasons.

If your puppy relieves stool five times a day or more, he may have worms, or he could be eating more than his body can digest. If this is the case, cut his food by 10 to 15 percent and check with your veterinarian. If your puppy is urinating eight to 10 times per day and is always thirsty, it is also time to check with your vet; the pup may have a urinary tract infection.

Step four in your house-training program is to set up a walk-and-play schedule. To be fair to a very young puppy (eight to 16 weeks), he should be taken out about every two or three hours, and a little less frequently as he ages and gains more bladder and bowel control. Puppies need to eliminate about 30 to 45 minutes after eating or drinking, after play sessions and immediately after waking from sleep.

First thing in the morning—6 A.M. is preferred for very young puppies—take the puppy from his crate and take him to his designated spot to relieve himself. The earlier you get the puppy outside, the less chance you will have a mess inside to clean up.

If the puppy relieves himself outside, allow him a little time to spend with you, on the leash, indoors. Between 6:30 and 7 A.M., feed him breakfast, preferably in his crate. About 45 minutes after feeding, take him outside to relieve himself; on the way out offer water. When he comes in, put him in the crate for a rest period.

At 11:30 A.M. take him out again. If he relieves himself, praise him and spend about 20 minutes with him. If he doesn't go, try again in 20 minutes or so.

The puppy should get another meal at 12:30. At about 1 P.M. offer water on the way out. If he relieves himself, play a bit afterward. Then put him back in the crate to nap.

About 4 P.M. give your puppy the last meal of the day and the last water. Then take him out at about 5 P.M. The last two walks of the day should be around 7 P.M. and 10:30 P.M. The later the better.

Of course, every home has a different routine, so use the above as a general guideline to set your own schedule based on your lifestyle. Furthermore, each puppy will have different requirements. A puppy with a lower activity level will probably not have to eliminate as often; whereas, a more nervous dog might have to go even more often.

In general, be careful that your puppy doesn't take in extra water by drinking from the toilet (put down the lid) or extra food by eating from cat food bowls, garbage cans, plates of food left around or anything else. If properly supervised, your puppy won't be able to get into any of these things.

IN CASE OF ACCIDENT . . .

Never reprimand your dog after a house-training accident. Enormous amounts of money have been spent studying how long after a behavior a dog can associate a correction with that behavior. The latest research suggests that a lapse of more than three seconds is too long for the dog to make a connection. So whether it is four seconds or 20 minutes after an accident, it is too late for your puppy to associate any correction with the action.

If you are properly supervising your puppy, he won't be able to make a mistake that you can't catch as it's happening. If you catch the puppy in the act, you can make a startling noise, but use an object, such as a book dropped on the floor, not your voice. This will usually make him constrict his bladder and bowel muscles. Then scoop him up and take him to where you want him to eliminate.

Do not use a cleaner with ammonia in it to clean up a mistake. To a dog, ammonia smells very similar to urine, and dogs like to eliminate in places where they've eliminated before. Instead, try white distilled vinegar or use one of the products on the market that is a pet-odor neutralizer.

PAPER TRAINING

Paper training can send conflicting messages to your dog. By allowing, even praising, elimination in the home (on paper or not), you can easily confuse your dog. One day you are telling him it is okay to go in the house, while the next day it isn't.

Still, there are times when people will choose to paper-train a dog. These usually include city apartment dwellers with small dogs and owners of very young puppies whose schedules do not permit them to walk the puppy as many times a day as is necessary. If that's the case in your home, it is unfair to leave a very young puppy in a crate all day—it is comparable to leaving a baby in the same diaper all day long.

If you must paper-train, choose one small area of your home, preferably a small bathroom. Check the room to make sure it is puppy-proofed, meaning there are no objects within the puppy's reach that could cause him harm. Cover the entire floor with a couple of layers of newspaper, and put the puppy in the room. Obviously, several times a day, clean up any paper the puppy has soiled. You don't ever want him to feel comfortable being in a dirty environment.

Every four to five days, remove a sheet of paper from the front of the bathroom, working your way toward the back of the room. This will teach the puppy to go toward the back of your bathroom, eventually on one piece of paper.

It is important to switch your dog to eliminating outside as soon as possible. Going indoors on paper should not become your puppy's lifestyle unless your dog is very small and/or you are unable to walk the dog often for medical reasons. By the age of four or five months, puppies should have better control of their bladder and bowels and should go directly to crate and house training.

At what age should a dog be fully house trained? This depends on how diligently you have helped him to learn the right habits. It also depends on his rate of maturity. Some dogs are almost fully mature at eight or nine months, while others are not really adults until two years of age.

We have seen many training guides that suggest house-training a young puppy can be accomplished in a few weeks. This is completely untrue. While it is possible to begin to build a habit of going in the right spot, namely outside, a puppy under four months old does not have adequate control of his bladder and bowel muscles to be given free reign of the house.

HOUSE TRAINING PROBLEMS

Pup messes in his crate. This could be caused by a number of things. The puppy may be ill, the crate may be too big, a towel may have been left in the crate, the puppy may have been left in the crate too long, or his routine may have been changed abruptly. First of all, make sure the puppy is healthy, showing no signs of abnormal stool or urine. Second, take out any towels or blankets, make sure the crate is the right size,

and stick to a fair and humane schedule of walks and feedings.

Pup finds hidden places to eliminate. This is usually the owner's fault. By allowing the puppy to roam out of sight, you are giving him the opportunity to make a mistake, so keep him on a leash and supervised at all times in the house until he is fully house trained. Also, if the puppy has had an accident in front of you before you may have yelled at him, which will probably make him want to hide from you when he needs to eliminate.

Even when we think we are supervising our puppies, we all take our eyes off them sometimes. So always be ready for an accident and have a distraction handy, such as a heavy book that you can drop on the floor to startle the puppy. He will probably constrict his bladder and bowels, at which point you should scoop him up and take him to where he should be eliminating. Remember, no hitting or yelling. You want the dog to associate the problem with the correction, not with you.

Pup eliminates inside after a walk. In this case he probably didn't relieve himself outside. You might want to try taking a little warm water out with you and rubbing it on his tummy to encourage urination. If that doesn't work, when you bring him back in, put him right back in his crate, then take him outside again about a half an hour later.

If a schedule is properly set up and followed, the chances of this happening are slim because you will be taking him outside when he really needs to eliminate.

Pup urinates when he's excited or when he greets people. This is called submissive urination or excited urination. It may be caused when a puppy is confused or is over-corrected, especially with verbal corrections. In this case he comes to associate corrections with that person, and urinates when the person is near to show that he is being submissive. If you think this is what is happening, be very careful not to use your voice to reprimand.

With both excited and submissive urination, get his mind off wetting and on to something else. Maybe give him a toy and keep walking past him. Don't make a big fuss over him with excited voices and lots of hand motions. Basically, don't overexcite or overstimulate him.

Pup won't eliminate when he's distracted. Don't walk around and around letting your puppy find "just the right spot." This makes it too easy to for him to focus on every fallen leaf and piece of litter that passes by. Instead, stay in one spot and don't talk to your puppy until he eliminates.

Your puppy may also be sound sensitive. You can help him become less sensitive by making distracting noises at home while he is playing and eating. Don't make so much noise that you frighten or upset him; just make enough to create a background sound that he can learn to filter out.

POTTY ON COMMAND

Establishing a word that cues your puppy to eliminate will be well appreciated on a cold rainy night when all you want is for your dog to hurry up! Go to the location you have chosen as your dog's "spot" when you know he has to go. When he begins to eliminate, say the word you have chosen (any word will do—some of our favorites are Hurry Up and Get Busy) and praise as the dog is relieving himself. After doing this a number of times, the word will become the cue for the act of eliminating.

SOCIALIZING YOUR DOG

What does socializing your dog mean? It means making your dog comfortable in a variety of situations. When dogs feel uncomfortable they may react by becoming stressed and over-anxious. In extreme cases they may growl or bite. If a dog is well socialized he will have the confidence to deal with a variety of circumstances.

The easiest time to socialize a dog is during puppyhood, mainly because you are starting from scratch. Your puppy should be exposed to as many people as possible. They should be of all races, ages and sizes. Try to make sure your puppy has a lot of positive encounters with men and children, because they are most often the recipients of dog bites.

Expose your puppy to as many situations as you can think up, including loud noises and crowds. And

Expose your puppy to other animals at a very young age if you expect him to be comfortable around them as an adult. Be sure to supervise at all times to make sure the puppy is learning what is acceptable and what is not.

if you expect your adult dog to behave in a relaxed manner around other animals, be sure to let him get used to them while he is still very young.

You should control these socialization experiences as much as possible. Remember, the goal of socializing your puppy is to make him feel confident and trusting in many situations. To do this, you must control his experiences and make sure they remain positive and instructive. Don't allow every person who walks by to run up to your puppy and start playing with him. Many people will think it is just fine to let your pup chew on their fingers and climb all over them. It doesn't matter if they don't mind—you should. This is your dog, and you're the one who will be living with him when he is an adult. It isn't fair to you or the puppy to allow other people to decide how he should behave.

Explain to people that your pup is learning how to greet people properly and how to enjoy their company. Have the puppy sit at your side to greet people.

Your puppy should meet lots of children, but these meetings should be positive experiences so your puppy learns to trust and respect children, not fear them. Teach the children how to handle a puppy before they say hello. This means you should explain to them how to respect the puppy's feelings. Rough play is inappropriate, and petting should be gentle.

The dog's individual character will determine the pace of socialization. Some dogs will naturally be more inclined to accept new situations with a calm demeanor, while others will require more time to adjust and feel comfortable. Watch your puppy's reactions, and be sensitive to when he's had enough.

PLAYING WITH YOUR PUPPY

One of the great joys of having a puppy is playtime. There are so many ways to have fun with your puppy! I don't want to rain on anyone's parade by telling them they can't play with their puppy in this way or that. Just remember that the games you play with your puppy will greatly affect how he behaves when it's not playtime.

A general rule of thumb is to stay away from games that nurture inappropriate behavior. If you don't want a dog who fights with you, then don't fight with

Some puppies do better when play is kept a bit calmer. Excited play can sometimes get out of hand and not every owner is capable of handling an over-excited puppy.

your puppy. Hard shoves, grabs and growling noises from you will be returned in kind by your puppy.

Your puppy's individual character should also help you choose how to play with him. A puppy with a strong, challenging character would probably be better off playing games where there is full cooperation between you both, such as fetch.

Some trainers suggest that nobody should play tug-of-war with their dogs. I disagree. For some dogs, if played properly, this game is fine. To be played properly, the game should be under your control at all times. When you choose to end it, you should be able to command the dog to release the object you're both tugging, and you should put it away. In this way you are establishing the fact that it is your property and you are only allowing the dog to play with it for a short period of time, as long as he follows your rules.

So have fun and play with your puppy, but watch for signs that he may be taking some games too far. If he is unwilling to relinquish toys, growls or otherwise behaves inappropriately, you should focus on regaining control of the situation by using the four basic commands that make up foundation training and on playing games that require him to obey and cooperate with you.

During the day you can leave any safe toys around for your pup to play with. Playing stimulates the puppy and may make him need to eliminate more frequently, so at night no toys after his last walk outside.

104

Keep a leash on the puppy for control. You don't want him to learn that he can run off with an object and hide from you, so don't let him get into the habit of doing so.

Once he has the toy in his mouth, encourage him to bring it back to you.

Offer lots of praise on his way back, and sometimes let him keep the toy for a bit while you calmly pet him.

HOW TRAINING SOLVES PROBLEMS

As with people, your dog's behavior is always changing. He may be perfect today, but a month from now a behavior may crop up that you find inappropriate. It is often difficult for owners to admit or to recognize when a behavior problem begins, let alone when it has become a habit. But the longer the behavior goes on the better chance it has of becoming ingrained. That's why it's important to deal with problems as soon as you notice them.

Specific problems will crop up with even the most well-trained dogs, but a dog who is not trained will have much more severe problems. That's why it's important to first get basic control of your dog by using foundation training.

Try not to label your dog as a "problem dog," because this only leads you to tolerate or even reinforce inappropriate behaviors. For example, the owner who says, "My dog is very fearful so I don't take him for walks" is only making this problem worse. Without adequate exposure to the world, the dog's fear will only intensify. Instead, this owner might approach the situation by saying, "My dog is afraid of some things. Let me figure out what they are and help him to overcome his fears." By taking control of the situation instead of avoiding it and just labeling the dog, you can enhance your dog's life by helping him to feel secure with you.

Always keep in mind that some behaviors, in both animals and people, may be due in part to a medical condition. It is important to consult your veterinarian to rule out the possibility of a medical problem causing a behavioral problem. Always treat the medical problem first, and then tackle the behavioral issue.

FORMING BETTER HABITS

We've already discussed how using foundation training consistently in real life helps your dog form good habits. You can also use this idea to teach your dog to substitute a good habit for a bad one. For example, if you have a dog who has a habit of jumping on people, you can teach him to Sit when he greets people. The behavior of sitting makes it impossible for the dog to jump. But since the act of jumping on people is a strongly formed habit, it will take a long time to develop the behavior of sitting to greet people into a habit just as strong. Most people don't stick to enforcing the new habit long enough, and the old habit is allowed to come back. Don't let that happen. Make sure your dog keeps up his good habits, and make sure you don't allow the bad ones to resurface.

You should definitely try to use real life situations for training, but sometimes, especially when treating specific behavior problems, you may need to set up situations in order to speed up the training process. If you want to teach your dog to greet people at the door by sitting, you don't really want to wait until enough friends stop by to visit. Instead, you may want to invite a few friends over to help you train your dog; maybe have them come to the door one by one on a certain day. By doing this, you are giving yourself and the dog a chance to work intensively on solving a particular problem.

In this chapter let's look at some of the most common behavior problems we see in dogs. They're arranged here alphabetically.

AGGRESSION

Aggression is a vast and complex component of animal behavior. There is aggression caused by dominance, fear, pain and instinct—maternal, predatory and territorial. Often, cases of aggression are an intricate mixture of several of these factors. Dog aggression can be directed towards humans or towards other animals.

All dogs have some aggression; it only becomes a problem when it is not contained to a degree that allows the dog and the people around him to live safely in the human world. That is, the dog must understand that it is unacceptable to show aggression to people unless he is being used specifically for police or protection work or is protecting his home or family.

There is some evidence that certain animals are genetically predisposed to higher levels of aggression and some aggression is caused by physiological or neurological disorders. However, the overwhelming percentage of dogs who have an aggression problem do not suffer from any disorder. Still, the first step in treating aggression is to talk to your veterinarian to rule out the possibility that the aggression is caused by a medical condition.

Most aggressive tendencies can be avoided or controlled if the proper socialization and training occurs in the animal's most formative weeks (five to 36 weeks). To socialize our animals, we must expose them to as many experiences as possible. This includes, but is not limited to, people of all ages, races and sizes, as well as various sights, sounds and activities. The key to keeping these experiences positive is to control them. For example, don't allow a child to play unsupervised with your new puppy, or any animal for that matter. You should be present to guarantee that both are following your predetermined rules of conduct.

When the young dog is comfortable in a wide variety of pleasant situations, you may be ready to move on to introducing him to some mildly aversive conditions. After all, we want our adult dog to feel confident in less than pleasant situations. For example, he may not enjoy rough petting, which is exactly the kind of thing that might elicit an aggressive response from an otherwise well-mannered dog. If we make him less sensitive to these kinds of things in puppyhood, aggression is less likely to play a major role in his adult personality.

Just as with people, aggression can be a partly learned behavior. If, as a puppy, a dog was encouraged by his human family to play rough wrestling games, they would probably be encouraging this puppy to react aggressively, at first to defend himself and then to test his strength. So be aware of what type of behaviors you are encouraging in your puppy.

Neutering or spaying your dog may help you and your dog avoid a problem with aggression. Sexual maturity in unneutered male dogs is the time when you are most likely to see a peak in aggressive behavior. A decrease in hormones as a result of neutering may help decrease certain types of aggression.

Most important, remember that just as all people have the capacity to feel happy, sad and angry, all dogs have the capacity to act aggressively. One of the reasons there are so many dogs in shelters is that many people do not accept this fact. A display of aggression does not always warrant labeling a dog as aggressive.

Dogs who behave aggressively are written off as bad, but in reality they simply have not been shown how to behave in our society.

If your animal is already exhibiting aggressive behavior, you must make a commitment to take control. This begins by making sure the dog is not in a position to hurt anyone. Then you need to seek professional help to learn how to handle the situation.

Most cases of aggression can be treated successfully by educating both the dog and his family. Success depends on how long the behavior has been allowed to develop and how committed the owners are to controlling it. Aggression problems are not usually cured, but they certainly can be controlled.

Treating aggression involves gaining control of the dog using foundation training and gaining control of the dog's environment to make sure he is living a lifestyle that will not feed his aggression. This can only be done with the help of a professional trainer, and you must contact one if aggression is a problem with your dog.

ALOOFNESS

By aloofness we mean a dog who is basically reserved and not focused on people. We do not mean a dog who is fearful. Aloofness can usually be avoided by properly socializing your dog when he is young. However, some dogs are naturally more reserved than others, and a reserved character is not necessarily a fault—unless, of course, you find it to be. In that case you must be fair to your dog and realize that while you can help him to form new habits, you cannot change his basic character.

If you want to encourage your aloof dog to be more outgoing, you must focus on rewarding him for even the smallest steps in the right direction. Obviously, keep your dog's preferences in mind when choosing rewards—it is only a reward if he sees it as such.

If he normally stays away when guests arrive, try having a visitor offer your dog a favorite treat. It is best if the treat is offered with little or no verbal coaxing from anyone, and the visitor should certainly not approach the dog. In fact, you should all ignore the dog. Don't make him feel he must interact with the visitor to get the treat, although that may come later if you go slowly. Repeating this situation often teaches the dog that being around people does not always require a lot of interaction on his part (this might take some of the pressure off) and is more often than not a highly rewarding experience.

BARKING AT VISITORS

It is a normal reaction for a dog to be protective of his territory and to bark at visitors. Most people actually appreciate a dog who lets them know that others are on their property. But this behavior gets annoying when the dog keeps barking after you have accepted these people into your home.

This problem is easy to solve by just having a leash on the dog and putting him on a Down command. In some cases this will be enough, because many dogs simply don't bark when they are lying down. If this doesn't take care of it, someone should step on the leash so he doesn't break the command, and another household member (only an adult) should stand behind the dog in a casual manner. Choose a command word, such as Quiet, and the person standing on the leash will say the word. The person behind will then throw a throw chain or bean bag at the dog's rump. As soon as the barking stops, pause for a few seconds and then calmly praise the dog. You are teaching him that the barking causes a negative.

If he barks again (which he will, because he is going to try to figure out what caused the negative), repeat the same process. The idea is not to hurt the dog, but simply to create an experience that's unfamiliar and a little uncomfortable. There should be absolutely no yelling or harsh voices used. Stay calm and quiet, and give your dog a chance to figure out the situation for himself.

If you don't have another household member to help, you can do it yourself by dropping the chain or bean bag on his rump from behind your back. Then praise the positive behavior of being quiet and let him deal with the negative on his own.

If your dog is a constant barker, the easiest and fastest solution is an anti-bark collar. These noise-sensitive collars emit a sound when the dog barks. There are other methods, but they are not as fast or effective.

Still, some dogs don't find the sound to be a strong enough negative to warrant being quiet. For them, there is a collar that emits a spray of citronella when the dog barks. Because most dogs are very sensitive to smells, this collar is very effective.

BARKING IN THE YARD

Barking when left alone in a yard is usually caused by boredom, territoriality, the visual stimulation of passing people and animals, or a combination of all of these. If your dog barks frequently in the yard, it will undoubtedly be considered a nuisance by your neighbors, but it may very well result in much more serious consequences. Your dog is vulnerable to being stolen, taunted or physically harmed by a passerby.

The best solution to this kind of barking may also prevent your dog from being harmed in some way: Don't leave him unsupervised in the yard for long periods of time. If you're not prepared to have a dog live in your house, you're not ready for a dog.

BITING

Dog bites are all too frequent in this country. This is due in large part to a lack of proper socialization and training for many dogs and the ignorance of many people. No dog can be "bite proofed," but your dog has a much better chance of getting through his life without a bite if you take control of him and of his environment. This means you must be sure people who come in contact with your dog have a basic understanding of how to treat dogs and how to behave around them. Don't allow anyone who taunts, harasses or otherwise unduly stresses your dog to be anywhere near him, especially if you aren't around.

Furthermore, as you become familiar with your dog's body language you will be able to watch for warning signs that he is becoming agitated. Don't assume that the only dogs who bite are large and are barking ferociously. Many bites are inflicted by dogs who are fearful and are lashing out in what they see as self-defense. So if your dog is signaling that he is uncomfortable with someone approaching him, by backing away for example, don't let that person push the issue.

You should also strongly consider spaying or neutering your dog; the Humane Society has reported that unneutered dogs are up to three times more likely to bite than neutered dogs.

A dog who bites as part of an overall pattern of aggression needs professional help. You cannot afford to ignore this problem, for your dog's sake and yours.

BOLTING THROUGH DOORS

You should be cautious about allowing your dog to get in the habit of bolting out the front door, whether on leash or off. When on leash he shouldn't pull, whether you're going down the street or through a door. A lot of people lose control of their dogs through doorways because they think it is all right for the dog to be excited on his way out. But remember, if you let him pull here, how is he supposed to know he can't pull when you're out on the street?

If you have a front or back yard and you let your dog out off leash, it can be very dangerous to let him bolt out the door. You can't be sure that a gate hasn't been left open or someone or something hasn't come into your yard. So try keeping him on a leash for a while and making him sit at the door until you release him. Use the Sit command whenever you open the door and your dog will get in the habit of sitting until you're ready to calmly lead him outside.

CAR TRAVEL

Many young dogs get carsick simply because they're not accustomed to car travel. You can help your dog by taking frequent short trips and building up to longer ones. Try not to schedule them after feeding times, especially if your dog has a habit of getting sick.

Lessen the anxiety your dog may feel in the car by taking some trips to places that your dog enjoys (most dogs are only in the car when taken to the vet or the groomer).

For your safety and your dog's, he should be restrained when traveling in the car. A crate is appropriate, but if you cannot fit a crate in your car, try tying your dog's leash to the seat belt or door handle. Commercial dog seat belts are available but are usually not a necessary investment.

Do not attempt to give your dog a command, such as Sit or Down, in the car. You will endanger yourself if he breaks the command and you have to turn around to replace or correct him.

Some dogs become very rambunctious when in a car. Restraining your dog in a crate is usually the best option in this case. You may also consider covering the crate with a towel or blanket so the dog is not so visually stimulated.

If your dog shows signs of being fearful of the car, again, the crate may be one of the best solutions. Be sure to train your dog to accept the crate (and, ideally, enjoy it) outside of the car first (see Chapter Seven for instructions on crate training). You may also want to try feeding your dog his meals in the car for a few weeks so he will begin to associate pleasant experiences with being in the car.

Never leave a dog in a car unattended, not even for a moment. It is common for dogs left alone in cars to be stolen or to suffer from heatstroke.

CHASING

Chasing is caused by the prey drive, which all dogs have, being allowed to develop into a habit. The chase instinct has been selectively bred to be very strong in certain breeds, but it can be curbed or contained. Obviously, the easiest solution is to supervise your dog and keep him on a leash. But if you are willing to take the enormous risk of letting your dog have access to things he can chase (which may get him or someone else hurt), the least you should do is minimize the chances of disaster.

To curb this behavior, the act of chasing has to produce a consistent negative. If your dog is chasing cars, allow the car to be the negative. If he's chasing bicyclists, they will be the negative. You yelling from the house probably won't interrupt the behavior, because his prey drive is too strong. With the help of a friend or neighbor, set up a situation where you can administer a correction. Have the other person drive by very slowly and as the dog approaches toss either a water balloon or five or six throw cans tied together at the dog. (Yes, this is a strong correction, but if your dog continues to chase cars he won't be around for long.) The dog's reaction will be, "Wow, that wasn't fun!"

Doing this just once won't work, especially if your dog has been chasing things for a long time and has formed a strong chasing habit. So don't leave him outside by himself where one day he could get away with chasing without a correction. If he does, that old habit will come flooding back.

CHEWING

First and foremost, do not leave your dog unsupervised in a room where he can do damage. Until you are absolutely sure your dog understands what he should and should not chew on, you must always have your eye on him.

If you are supervising your dog and you see him begin to chew something inappropriate, stay calm. If you use your voice to yell at him all you will do is make your dog fear you. He will probably stop chewing things when you are around, but he will quickly learn that if you aren't in the room chewing is all right.

Find a light object nearby, and toss it at your dog's rear end in a very non-emotional way. Don't fling it angrily, don't make eye contact and, most important, don't say a word. You want your dog to believe that objects come flying at him out of nowhere when he chews on certain things.

After the correction, he will stop chewing for a moment. Then he will probably hesitantly go back to chewing. Toss another light object. Usually after the second correction the dog will only glance back at what he was chewing and decide not to try it again. He has made the connection that chewing that particular object is what caused something to drop onto his rear.

Be sure to provide your dog with an adequate supply of appropriate chew toys to redirect his need to chew.

DEMANDING ATTENTION

Catering to your dog's every whim is unfair to both of you. While his pleading glances may be sweet, you should not encourage him to believe he is in a position to demand anything from you. This will inevitably lead to problems such as destructive behavior, because he will begin to believe he is in a position to set the rules.

To solve this problem, use the commands Sit and Down. If you are on the phone and the dog starts to pester you for attention, put him on a Down. Then, a few moments later, you can praise him and let him know that being in that position, not begging for attention, is how he gets praise and attention.

DESTRUCTIVE BEHAVIOR

Most people believe destructiveness is caused by spite. But, as discussed in a previous chapter, spite is a learned human emotion—one your dog cannot experience. More often than not, destructive behaviors are caused by some combination of boredom, stress and opportunity (that soft slipper was lying on the floor, so why shouldn't I chew it?).

If your dog already has a habit of destructiveness, then you must make sure you don't allow him anymore opportunities. Confine him in a crate when you are unable to supervise him. This is for your own good and for his, because destructive behavior often leads to dogs hurting themselves by chewing electrical cords or eating dangerous materials from the garbage, for example.

Deal with boredom and stress by spending more time calmly teaching your dog lifestyle training. When you catch him in a destructive act, administer your corrections calmly using the techniques you learned in Chapter Five.

DIGGING

Dogs dig because it is a natural doggy behavior. They dig to bury food, to make dens for puppies, to find warmth in the cold weather and cool earth in the warm weather and for plain old fun. You have two options in regard to your dog and digging: You can choose never to allow him to dig, or you can provide your dog with his own digging area.

If you go with the first option, the dog must not be allowed to spend unsupervised time in your yard. If you allow him out there when nobody is watching, he will have ample opportunity to dig and further reinforce this habit. If he digs even while you supervise him, try keeping him on a leash for control or using a throw can to correct while he is digging. And remember that corrections after the fact are useless and unfair to your dog.

If you recognize that digging is a very natural doggy behavior that you are willing to put up with, you may want to try option number two. The idea is similar to a child's sandbox. Choose one designated area of your yard, take your dog over to that area and encourage him to dig there. He may be hesitant to dig in front of you if you have yelled at him for this behavior in the past. Dig a little yourself and try burying a few treats or maybe a toy or a bone. Praise when he joins in.

Keep in mind that even though you are showing your dog that he may dig in this area, it doesn't mean he won't try to dig in other areas. So you must still supervise him while he is in the yard.

EATING AND ROLLING IN FECES

As disgusting as this habit may seem to you, it is a very natural, common behavior for dogs. In fact, there's even a word for it—coprophagy. No one is really sure why dogs eat their feces. It may be that something is lacking in the dog's diet, or the dog may have worms or simply be hungry.

Whatever the cause, veterinarians agree the habit does not promote good health. And the solution is clear: Don't give your dog the opportunity to continue this habit. That means don't leave him unsupervised in the yard, especially just after he has relieved himself. Pick up and dispose of his feces promptly.

You might also try talking to your vet to see if you can feed your dog a bit more food, or at least spread his current quantity out over more feedings. So if he is eating three cups of food a day (one and a half in the morning and one and a half in the evening), you might switch to one cup in the morning, one cup around noon and one cup around 4 p.m.

EXCESSIVE ATTACHMENTS

Dogs can become excessively attached to people and to objects. Excessive attachment to people is usually the result of an unsound temperament. This is exacerbated when the dog is not properly socialized, allowing this tendency to be unsure and fearful to develop.

Owners should be careful to make sure every puppy spends time by himself and with different people, whether or not he enjoys it at first. You never know which puppy will develop into an overly attached dog, so it is better to err on the side of caution with all puppies.

Excessive attachment to objects is usually a possessive act. The dog believes he can keep whatever he gets by displaying aggression or by running away with the object. Again, this is usually a result of allowing a tendency in a dog's character to develop into a habit. When you give your puppy or dog a toy to play with, remind yourself and him that the object is really yours and that you are just lending it to your dog. Until you are sure your dog will release objects to you without showing aggression, keep him on a leash in the house so you have control. Do not allow him to take items and run off to hide with them. Instead, encourage him, with the help of the leash, to play with you and the object together.

EXCITABILITY

Highly excitable dogs have usually been bred for high-intensity work and do not have enough activity to keep them occupied at home. These dogs need discipline, and you must teach them to think before they react. Dogs who react without thinking are very excitable, much like a child running toward a playground—they are so caught up in the idea of getting there as fast as possible that they aren't really thinking.

Thinking will calm your dog. It is like us driving up to a Stop sign. It forces us to stop and think for a moment before we drive on. Think of commands as

Stop signs for your dog. They help him to pause and consider his actions.

With puppies and adolescent dogs, be careful not to inadvertently encourage overexcitable behaviors. You might want to tone your own behavior down a bit in order to help your dog do so.

FEAR

Fear, like most behavior problems, can have complex causes and therefore needs complex treatments. However, some general rules do usually apply. First and foremost, do not coddle your dog when he is fearful. Most owners pander to dogs who are fearful, hoping that reassuring the dog will make him feel better. Two things happen when you do this: First, the dog is being praised and encouraged for fearful behavior. It is difficult for a dog to distinguish reassurance from praise, and he will continue to act fearfully because he is being told that is the right thing to do. Second, the dog will come to rely on his owners' coddling. But what will happen when there is no one there to coddle him? He may go into a deeper panic.

The second general rule is that you shouldn't attempt to force your dog into a situation when he is truly fearful. If he is showing slight hesitation due to fear (for example, if he is learning to walk down stairs), this is very different than if he is truly panicked, such as if a firecracker goes off near him.

A properly socialized and well-trained dog will feel confident in the majority of situations you put

him in. But all dogs will experience periods of fear, just as people do. You may see your dog as a very confident animal, but this doesn't mean he won't have his moments, as we all do. How often he feels fearful is influenced by a number of factors, including age, genetics, hormones and stress. The important thing is to handle these situations in such a way that you let your dog know he will be all right as long as he looks to you for guidance. This doesn't mean that he should cower at your side, but that you will give him instructions and he will be okay if he listens to you.

Obedience commands are a wonderful tool for overcoming fear. You have taught your dog that when he obeys the commands Sit or Down, only good things happen. So when you see the dog is behaving a little fearfully, give a command and then praise. This also helps the dog refocus on something other than what he is afraid of.

In moments of mild fear you can encourage your dog to investigate the object or situation by pretending to pay no attention to his fear and investigating the object yourself. For example, if you are walking down the street and your dog balks at a bag of garbage, walk over to it casually and just pat it with your foot until the dog realizes that since you aren't afraid, he need not be.

If your dog is already experiencing high levels of fear, you can try to desensitize him to the object(s) of his fear. You do this by exposing the dog to low levels of the stimulus that is causing the fear. At the

This dog seems to be truly fearful at this woman's approach. It is unfair to everyone to allow this sort of situation to go on. The dog may be so afraid that he will lash out at the woman in order to keep her away.

same time, occupy the dog with things that he finds pleasurable, such as food, attention from you, playing with another dog or obedience commands. Gradually increase the level of the stimulus. This process associates the stimulus that caused fear with things the dog finds pleasurable.

Desensitization is often successful with dogs that fear car travel (feeding them in the car is the positive associated with the stimulus) and loud noises (audio tapes of loud noises are played at low levels when the dog is eating and playing and the volume is gradually increased).

FEAR OF THE VET

It is understandable for a dog to be fearful when visiting a veterinarian's office. It is an environment with

117

Playing vet at home is a great way to make real visits less stressful for everyone.

mock exam with the help of another household member or friend.

Also, take your dog to a lot of different places and practice long Downs in all of them. This way, when you go to the vet's office you can put him on a Down and he will feel more comfortable responding to a command he is familiar with. Also, take a few treats to the vet's office to give as a bonus when he is on the Down command.

GARBAGE RAIDING

Dogs raid garbage pails for some very obvious reasons: They are searching for bits of food and/or they are bored and scavenging is a way to occupy time. Obviously, searching for food is a very natural doggy behavior, but it is inappropriate at home because the dog may find something in the garbage that is dangerous if swallowed, such as chicken bones or pieces of metal or other toxic substances. Furthermore, in his search through the garbage the dog will inevitably make a mess by spreading the garbage around on the floor.

The best solution to this problem is prevention. Invest in garbage pails that are covered and, even better, pails that can be locked shut. A crate can also prevent your dog from having the opportunity to go on raiding missions while you are away from home.

There are some garbage cans that you may not want to lock shut (such as small bathroom pails).

some very strange sounds and smells and a place where the dog rarely experiences any positives. But you can make visits to the vet less stressful for you and your dog, which will make your vet's job a lot easier.

To begin, play veterinarian at home with your puppy or dog. Find a surface that is similar to the exam table at your vet's office (slippery), and do a

If you catch your dog in the act of raiding these, do not yell at him—you'll only teach him not to raid the pails when you are around. Your goal is to teach him that he should avoid the pails at all times, whether you are around or not.

You will teach your dog that it is not in his best interest to sniff in the trash by booby trapping the cans so that they correct him, not you. You have a few options for how to do this. If you are nearby, you can toss a light object at the dog when his nose is in the pail. This is not meant to cause any pain, but rather to startle the dog and associate putting his nose in the can with an unpleasant feeling. When administering this correction you must do your best to disassociate yourself. So don't make a sound and avoid eye contact with your dog when he looks around to see what is happening. You should act as surprised as he is.

Another option is to purchase the smallest mouse trap you can find and place it in the bottom of the pail, covered with some newspaper. When the dog puts his nose in the pail he will be startled by the snap. Remember, the trap is not meant to actually catch the dog's nose—that is why you should use only a very small trap and carefully cover it adequately with paper. You may want to smear a bit of a tasty substance on the paper to encourage your dog to investigate.

One correction is not a cure—especially if your dog already has a long-established habit of garbage raiding—so you may need to set up these corrections a number of times. But being consistent with the new habit will overthrow the old habit.

Remember, never correct garbage raiding after the fact. Your dog will not associate the punishment with the act, and all you will accomplish is to make your dog afraid of you.

GREETING OTHER DOGS

To assume all dogs must say hello to each other on the street is unrealistic. Not every dog will get along with every other dog. Furthermore, if you allow your dog to approach every dog he sees on the street, he can hardly be expected to have his attention on you. When he is on the alert to see who is headed his way, he will most probably be straining at the end of a tight leash as well.

If you would like your dog to interact with other dogs when you walk him, be selective. The most important factor is that you, not your dog, should choose who he greets. If you don't want him to approach another dog, use the Come command and walk on by.

When your dog does go up to say hello to another dog, don't tense the leash. You must allow the dogs to examine each other as naturally as possible. If you pull back on the leash, you will be breaking the natural body postures dogs use to communicate and you may make your dog feel protective of you. You may even inadvertently cause a dog fight.

By allowing your dog to charge up to other dogs on the street, you are telling him that it is appropriate for him to pull you and to decide what he should pay attention to.

Make sure you have your dog under control around other dogs. You should decide if they can safely play together.

HEEL NIPPING

Nipping at the heels is often redirected herding behavior. Dogs use this behavior to control animals much larger than themselves, such as cattle. This is a natural instinct some dogs transfer from livestock to people. It is most likely not a dangerous behavior, but a child could get hurt by a dog nipping as he runs and plays.

As the dog is in the act of chasing and nipping, provide a correction from a throw can or chain, or a leash correction with the dog on a long leash. This way the heel nipping is what causes the negative, not you.

Heel nipping can also take the form of a shy, biting dog who nips at the back of legs when people walk away from him. This is not derived from the herding instinct, it is an act of aggression and should never be tolerated. To teach your dog that this behavior is unacceptable, have him on a leash. Get lots of people to walk by (preferably with heavy pants on—and no children). As the dog goes to nip, snap the leash sharply three or four times in a row. When he comes back to you, praise. Make him think that any time he goes after a heel there is a negative consequence.

HOUSE SOILING

Chapter Seven discusses house training for puppies, including how to deal with most house training problems. But adults can also sometimes have accidents. When a house trained adult is soiling indoors, the problem can have many causes. These include illness, medication (steroids, for example, can lead to frequent urination), lack of training, submissive urination and marking. However, the main reason that a dog eliminates in the house is that he has to go and wasn't given enough opportunities to go outside.

Be sure to have your dog checked by your veterinarian to eliminate the possibility that this is a medical problem, such as a urinary tract infection, parasites, incontinence due to age or something else. If there is a medical problem, have that treated first before you tackle the dog's behavior. It is unfair and even cruel to correct a dog for soiling in the house if he is physically unable to control himself.

Also, determine whether you are giving your dog adequate opportunities to relieve himself. Many times clients have called to say they believe their dog is eliminating in the house on purpose because he's mad that they leave him to go to work. After a few minutes of conversation it usually comes out that the dog is only being walked twice a day (before and after work). I'm sure they would have a hard time too if they were only permitted to go to the bathroom twice a day!

A well-timed schedule and supervising your dog are the keys to solving house-soiling problems. This means that you schedule the appropriate number of walks at the appropriate times. You will determine how many walks are appropriate based on your dog's age and health. Generally, the younger the animal, the more walks he will need. Older dogs will also need more frequent walks. The appropriate times are based on when the dog is fed and on your schedule.

Your dog should be walked approximately one hour after he is fed. On average, an adult dog needs at least three or four walks a day. Crate your dog to help him build bladder and bowel muscle control. After he has eliminated outside, he can have supervised play-times inside.

Even if you have a yard, it is not advisable to allow a dog to go into the yard by himself to eliminate. Unless you're watching, you can't be sure if he has gone, so you may let him back in the house still needing to eliminate.

Don't punish mistakes made in the house—this will only make matters worse. Physical and verbal punishments will not teach the dog where to eliminate. They will only make the dog fearful of you and may even teach him to eliminate behind the couch because you don't like to see him do it. Then when you have him on a leash outside he may be afraid to go in front of you.

If you catch him in the act, you can make a loud noise using something other than your voice, such as a book dropped on the floor. This should startle your dog, making him constrict his bladder and bowel muscles. Then you can rush him outside and praise him for going in the right spot.

If there is a mistake, clean it up with a commercial product that contains a bacterial enzyme odor eliminator or with distilled white vinegar. Don't use anything with ammonia in it, because this smells like urine to dogs.

HOWLING

Many dogs howl or bark constantly when left alone, in the house or in the yard. This habit will undoubtedly do more to create anti-dog feelings in your neighborhood than anything else.

Prevention is the best option; don't teach your young dog to expect attention and human companionship all the time. You should confine your dog for short periods several times a day (preferably in a crate), even when people are bustling around the house. If he cries while confined in the crate, ignore it for a few minutes and then toss a throw can at the crate. (Chapter Seven has more information on crate training.)

Obedience training will develop control and communication between you and your dog. Use the Down command if your dog is pestering you for attention and he will eventually learn to relax and be quiet when he's not receiving your attention.

If howling has already turned into a habit for your dog, you may need to use a training collar that will automatically administer a correction each time your dog vocalizes, even if you aren't around. There are a number of such collars on the market. The most successful is the ABS collar, which uses a squirt of citronella as the negative when the dog howls or barks. This is a completely humane method of correction. The dog's keen sense of smell is what makes this device so effective.

Toss a throw can at the door of your dog's crate to help him learn to settle down.

HYPERACTIVITY

Dogs who behave in a wild or rambunctious manner are often referred to as hyperactive. First, consult your veterinarian to rule out the possibility that this is a neurological disorder, although this is rare. Also, consult with him or her about the best diet for your dog. Certain ingredients in foods may affect your dog's behavior, and high levels of protein are not always advisable for the average pet dog as they may provide him with too much energy.

Just giving a lot of exercise to a hyperactive dog is not enough. They will build up more strength and be more fit and therefore have more energy. It is just as important, if not more important, for the dog to be mentally exercised. Allow your dog to think. Set rules and use commands to help enforce them. For example, teach him to Sit and use the command in real life by having him sit to greet people. The more clear you are about what you expect, the better, because an anxious dog is a confused dog, and a confused dog is more likely to be out of control.

Instead of yelling at your dog if he runs circles around your living room, place him on a five-minute Down. By clearly establishing an alternative to running wild, you will be humanely showing your dog what behaviors you consider to be right and you will be able to enjoy your energetic pet in a calmer way.

After two or three corrections, this puppy will associate the act of jumping on people with the negative experience of something hitting his rear.

He is immediately shown a behavior that will result in a positive experience—sitting to greet people.

JUMPING ON FURNITURE

If your dog is on the furniture and you don't want him to be, you need to supervise him at all times when he is around the prohibited furniture. Get behind the furniture and use your throw chain or bean bag for a correction, and get your dog in the habit of lying down on his own blanket or mat on the floor when you are on the couch.

JUMPING ON PEOPLE

One of the reasons dogs jump is to get closer to your face—to greet you and be friendly. So with puppies, crouch or bend down and help them to sit to say hello from the very beginning and they'll never get into the habit of jumping on people.

If your dog is already jumping, the two simplest and most effective methods to stop this habit are teaching your dog to Sit to greet people and using the walk through. For the first method, Sit to greet, have your dog on a leash until you have firmly established this new habit. Any time someone wants to greet your dog, have the dog Sit. He should be praised for being in that position. Be sure to say the Sit command before he begins to jump, not as he is doing it.

If your dog is very fast or active, try the walk-through method. As the dog is jumping, look straight above him. Don't make any eye contact or say anything, and march straight ahead. You are teaching the

The act of jumping causes Fabian to march straight forward through the dog. After a few times the dog will realize the only result of jumping on Fabian is a negative one.

dog that when he jumps on you he does not get the attention he's looking for; instead, you will charge forward over him.

The first time you do this the dog will be startled. The second time he will start thinking about the connection between his jumping and your detached

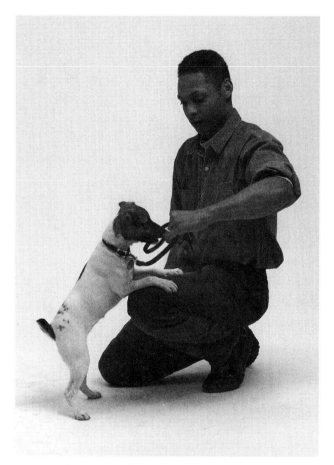

You can also use a leash to correct the dog with a snap sideways for jumping on you.

Do not use your voice to say anything to the dog when correcting.

Help him into a Sit and praise.

behavior. The third time he will put the blame on the act of jumping. When his feet are on the ground, have him Sit and praise him.

Be sure everyone in the household is consistent with this. If there are little children, they should not try the walk through, because the dog could knock them over. Rather, he should be on a leash and you should be there to snap it as a correction. If you have someone to help you can also try tossing a light object at the dog's rear when he is in the process of jumping.

LICKING

Licking is a friendly greeting, and some people don't think dog licks are a problem. If you don't mind but your visitors do, just put the dog on a Down away from them.

If, on the other hand, you and the rest of your household don't like it, simply don't let your puppy develop the habit. Be fair and establish rules in puppyhood. Use a leash correction, and snap the leash to the side two or three times. When your pup comes up to you and doesn't lick, offer lots of praise.

Licking is a friendly greeting, and some owners enjoy their dog's kisses.

If you don't have a leash on the dog and he comes over to lick you, just get up in an abrupt manner and walk right through him. Make no eye contact, and praise only when he walks over and doesn't lick you. You are teaching your dog that licking causes you to walk away.

MOUNTING

This problem is usually more prevalent in dogs with a dominant disposition. Mounting is a way dogs express their dominance, and unchecked it can lead to a dog who tries to be in control of you. This is a very dangerous habit, especially if there are kids around.

Treat mounting with a walk through or leash corrections, or have someone behind you administer a throw correction. After the correction, put the dog in a Down to reinforce your dominant position over him.

MULTI-DOG HOUSEHOLDS

Many people call four or five weeks after bringing a second dog into their home because they are unhappy with the resulting situation. The first question I usually ask is, "Why did you get a second dog?" The answer is almost always the same: "To keep my first dog company."

People who get a second dog for this reason are usually the ones who regret it most. Adding a dog to your household is a more difficult transition than most people are prepared for. The second dog is often accused of "ruining" the first, introducing bad habits and instigating fights. This is almost always unfair, and what is going on is far more complex.

A dog who lives only with humans is more likely to learn human rules of interaction and behavior. Humans are all he has, so he has to fit himself into their world. But in a two-dog household, the dogs have each other and canine behavior is much more compelling to a dog than human behavior. So it will be a difficult fight against nature to get your dogs' attention.

Just as it is more difficult to teach two birds living together to speak, it is often more difficult to successfully domesticate two or more dogs living together. They will respond more readily to the rules of other dogs if you aren't careful. Being too strongly dog-oriented and displaying natural dog behaviors too prominently is what often gets dogs in multi-dog households into trouble.

This is not to say that some families don't run beautifully with more than one dog. But you should add more canine members to your family because you want them, not because you suspect your dog does. You acquired a dog to keep you company, and if you don't have the time to keep him from getting lonely, you certainly won't have the time for a second dog. Two dogs require twice as much time, not half as much.

If, after careful consideration, you decide to bring home another dog, be sure to choose a dog whose character will be compatible with both you and your first dog. So for example, don't bring home a very aggressive dog if your current dog is very mild.

Introduce the dogs in a neutral setting, meaning outside of either dog's territory. It would be unfair and potentially dangerous to bring another dog into your first dog's territory and expect the first to readily accept the situation.

The introduction should be as low-key as possible. Any people involved should stay calm and try to have as few family members there as possible—your dog may become protective of you. Don't try to force either dog to say hello. Rather, let them check each other out when they are ready.

If your dogs spend more time with each other than with you, they will develop a very strong pack mentality. But this is your environment, and you want them to understand that they must respect each other in your space. You would set down the house rules for children and not allow them to set their own rules—the same applies to your dogs.

When the dogs are outside playing on their own time they can establish a pecking order. But try not to let them get into conflicts with each other. One fight can lead to consistent fighting.

PUPPY NIPS

We're not talking here about serious aggression, which must be dealt with professionally, but about puppy nips. There seem to be many people who consider it quite normal for a puppy to use human hands as a teething toy. This is absolutely not the case. Puppies do need to teethe, and puppies will use their teeth in games with other puppies, but under no circumstances should any puppy be allowed to teethe on

Fabian is letting the puppy figure out that he shouldn't bite human hands because it causes an uncomfortable feeling in his mouth.

human hands. Your puppy must learn from the moment he comes into contact with humans that it is unacceptable to place his teeth on any part of a human being.

The two traditional methods for dealing with this are to get angry and say "no!" or to hold his muzzle shut and say "no bite!" The problem with these two methods is that you run the risk of making the puppy afraid of people and uncomfortable with people putting their hands anywhere near his mouth. Instead, we want our puppy to like to be around

us and to be comfortable having people touch his muzzle.

The right way to deal with puppy bites is to remain as calm as possible and leave your hand in the puppy's mouth. Put your thumb on his tongue and press down firmly until he shows signs of being a little uncomfortable and trying to spit your thumb out. It is crucial that you do not say anything to the puppy or glare at him. It is your job to act as if you have no idea what is going on. When he spits out your thumb, continue to calmly play with him and pet his face gently.

He will learn that the act of biting you is what caused the discomfort in his mouth, not you.

Remember, puppies do need to teethe, and adult dogs need to chew all their lives in order to maintain healthy teeth and gums. Make sure your dog has things that are appropriate to chew on.

Puppy nipping is not a bad behavior—it is natural. Dogs are doing what they are programmed by nature to do. Our job is simply to teach them how to develop in a different way to get along and survive in our society.

RUNNING AWAY

If your dog gets loose and doesn't respond to your call, don't chase him. If you do, he is likely to continue to run out of fear or because he may view the situation as a chase game.

Instead, bend down and pretend you are investigating something very interesting on the ground. Then hold it out as though it were a treat you had just found for him. This may pique his curiosity and encourage him to come closer to you to check things out. When he gets near, don't reach for him unless you are sure you can get hold of him. Instead, avert your eyes, pretend you are holding something and bring it close to you, to lure your dog in even closer. Then get hold of him.

After one runaway incident, you should be very enthusiastic about training for a Come command that will work under even the heaviest distractions.

Many people play games of tag with young puppies. These games encourage the habit of running away, so it's best to avoid them. Instead, work on teaching a solid recall from day one. If your dog understands clearly how pleasurable it is to come to you, but that running away is negative, he will be much less likely to ever run off.

THE PICKY EATER

A picky eater may be attempting to train you to feed him exactly what he wants exactly when he wants it. Don't allow this behavior to even start. Set a time limit (about 15 minutes) for the food to be down, then pick it up, even if he hasn't finished it. No dog ever starved from missing one meal.

POSSESSIVENESS

Possessiveness is a behavior that is primarily conditioned by nature, because in the wild, to possess is to survive. Your dog is not doing it because he doesn't like you; he just hasn't been taught yet that it is unacceptable in our society. But in the domestic setting it can become very dangerous, especially if children are involved.

Possessiveness is usually a problem in dominant dogs who have been allowed to develop this tendency. It is most often displayed by guarding food or objects.

The best way to deal with possessiveness is to curb it early on. Give your puppy objects and then take them away often. If your puppy is possessive over anything, you should take it away. If he growls at your approach or when you reach to take it, give a sharp leash correction or use the throw can or throw chain.

You must try not to be emotional when giving this or any other correction.

If the behavior is already developed, you may want to use a pinch collar for a correction—but remember never to use your voice. Keep the dog on a leash and collar at all times until this habit is curbed. You do that by conditioning the dog to accept when things are taken away from him. Snap the leash until he leaves the item, then give it back, then repeat. Don't give him anything unless you are in a position to take it away. That means if he is off leash (he shouldn't be), he should have nothing to play with that he can possess, or else you will be feeding the old habit.

Play games with him where giving things up means the game goes on, while refusing to puts an end to the game. Seek the help of a professional if the dog shows aggression.

PROTECTIVE BEHAVIOR

There is nothing wrong with a dog being protective of his family or his environment. It is only bad if the protective behavior supersedes the control you have over your dog. For example, if a stranger comes to the door it is fine for the dog to be protective, but it is not okay if you give him a command to settle him and his protective instinct overrides the command.

Lifestyle training, that is, using the foundation commands in real life and consistently enforcing them, will eventually control this bad habit.

SEPARATION ANXIETY

Many owners unintentionally create a situation where their dog is uncomfortable when he's not in their presence. This happens when the owner gives the dog an enormous amount of attention. This can make the dog feel abandoned when the owner leaves and anxious in anticipation of the exciting return.

To deal with this problem, start by keeping your arrivals home very low key. When you walk in the door don't make any verbal or eye contact with your dog for at least the first few minutes. Put him in a Down and greet him after he's settled down. In time, it will become habit for the dog to relax and lie down when you come home, so anticipating your arrival won't be as stressful.

Be sure to spend time at home without paying attention to your dog. He must learn to be on his own, even while you are home. When you leave, be as calm as you are when you arrive home. Play around with the routine of your departure. Every once in awhile go out the door and come back in after a minute or two. This will help alleviate your dog's fears that when you leave it is always for a very long time.

SNIFFING

This usually refers to dogs sniffing guests, and is not easily dealt with, because dogs have to sniff by nature.

It is one of the main ways they come to know the world around them. Don't make a big deal out of it, just put the dog on a Down—that is what the training is for. You shouldn't get into the habit of thinking every behavior needs a correction.

STEALING

If your dog has a habit of stealing objects off counters and table tops, you should not have to interact with the dog or give him a command to stop. If you do this the dog will only learn that he should not steal when you are watching him. Instead, arrange things so that the dog gets a correction from the table, counter or object he is attempting to steal. In this way he will clearly associate the negative with the object being stolen and decide that it is not a rewarding experience.

Place a piece of meat on the counter tied with string to a pitcher of water. When the dog steals the meat he will pull the water down on himself. You run in to save him. If the dog is not very sensitive, tie the meat to throw cans instead of water. Build a tower of cans that will come tumbling down.

If the dog steals an object off the floor, such as a shoe, casually toss a light throw object (a throw can or chain) at the dog's rump. Make him think the correction comes from his action, not from you. Do not pick up the item he was chewing. We want him to decide that it is undesirable to chew it. You will probably have to repeat this correction two or three times until the dog makes a clear connection between chewing the object and the correction.

SUBMISSIVE BEHAVIORS

These behaviors can range from submissive body postures to submissive urination and are most likely genetically based. However, a tendency to be submissive is exacerbated when a dog is under-socialized and lacks confidence. This can become dangerous, because the lack of confidence may lead to fear aggression.

Try to socialize your dog by taking him for lots of calm walks. Training will help to build his confidence, but it is most likely that these behaviors will never completely go away.

Many people confuse submissive or appeasement gestures with guilt. When they come home to find the dog has gone on a garbage raid in the kitchen they may gasp at the sight of the mess on the floor. The dog can sense the change in the owner and may act submissive in an effort to avoid a conflict. This is a dog's way of saying, "Don't hurt me, I submit, I give in."

The owner is understandably upset with the situation, even more so because she thinks the dog "knows" he was bad. In reality, the dog cannot associate anything he did even a minute ago with himself. Dogs simply don't remember things in the same way we do. So his gestures have nothing to do with the very human emotion of guilt.

An environment in which a dog is confused and verbally reprimanded will certainly exacerbate submissive behaviors. For example, if you come home to find your dog has soiled the carpet and you yell at him, he probably won't understand why you are yelling. However, he will be fearful and may urinate as an act of submission and appeasement.

Keep the dog on leash for control and do not get emotional with the dog when you know he is prone to urinate submissively. Make very little eye contact at these times; you want to let the dog develop a different way of seeing you. Use the commands Sit and Down to keep his mind busy and to make him more confident (this way he'll know what you want from him and will be able to do it).

If your dog seems to be urinating frequently, have your vet check him to make sure there is no medical problem such as a urinary tract infection.

WHINING

Dogs whine mainly due to stress and conflict, such as when they are in a new environment. This should be dealt with in the same way you would deal with a dog who constantly barks or howls. Try to ignore the behavior for a few moments. Place the dog on a Down. By putting him on a command, you are giving him something to think about other than his stress.

Be careful not to feed the behavior by coddling your dog and telling him everything will be all right. This will only be interpreted as praise for whining.

REAL LIFE

Throughout this book we've talked about training your dog in real-life situations. It's impossible to underplay the importance of this. The way you interact with your dog every day and all the time dictates what he will learn and how well he will learn it.

The applications of real-life training may not always seem obvious. The way you handle everyday activities, such as feeding and grooming, for example, have a strong impact on many aspects of your dog's behavior.

FEEDING

The time of feeding and the way in which the dog is fed are crucial. Dogs who are allowed free access to food throughout the day may have a more difficult time controlling their bowel movements, and this affects house training. It is advisable to schedule feedings one to three times a day, depending on your dog's age, health and temperament. Consult your veterinarian about the best feeding schedule.

The food bowl should be left down for no more than 20 minutes. It is crucial that you not allow your dog to demand food. Owners who encourage this behavior are also encouraging the dog to believe he has control over them. This can lead the dog to test his control in other ways, as well.

The type of food you feed your dog is vitally important to his physical and mental health. Many dogs that are referred to trainers labeled as "hyperactive" are easily "cured" through training and by modifying the dog's diet with the help of a veterinarian. Many commercial dog foods contain a high level of protein and other ingredients that can effect your dog's temperament. Just as with people, you are what you eat. Consult your vet to make sure you are feeding your dog the best diet possible.

CHEWING

It is a dangerous myth that dogs must have access to animal bones. While it is true that they should be able to regularly chew on something to keep their teeth

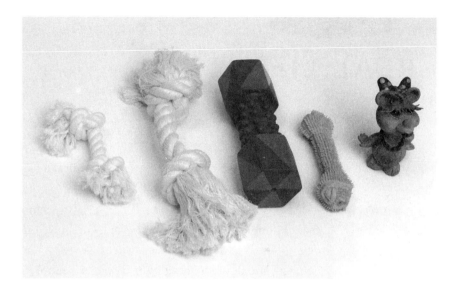

Your dog needs safe chew toys that are the right size for him.

and gums healthy, your choice of what they may chew is very important.

You should never give your dog poultry or pork bones because they can easily splinter in the dog's mouth or intestines. Even large cow bones can be dangerous. You are better off buying some tough nylon or sterilized rawhide bones.

GROOMING

It is essential that your dog willingly accept grooming, not only for his hygiene but also for reasons of basic control and safety. If you are unable to examine and touch every part of your dog's body without a struggle, it will be impossible to do so in an emergency. If your dog injures his paw and the vet must examine it, your dog will be less likely to receive prompt care if he panics at having his paw touched. So even if your dog has a short coat, you should still regularly groom him to get him used to being touched all over.

A thorough grooming consists of cleaning the dog's coat, ears, teeth, clipping nails and doing a routine check for any new lumps or bumps that might signal a health concern.

There is no need to constantly bathe your dog. Some coat types do not do well with frequent bathing, which may strip your dog's coat of natural oils. A good brushing will stimulate the skin. Ask your veterinarian how often your dog should be bathed.

Many people can't clip their dog's nails because they put up such a struggle. But your dog can be taught from puppyhood to relax during this process.

Be sure to thoroughly brush your dog's teeth to avoid serious health problems.

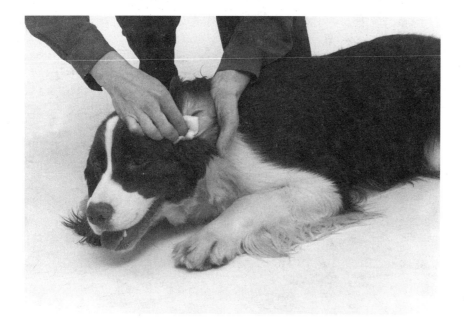

Gently wiping your dog's ears with a cotton swab will help to prevent ear infections.

EXERCISE AND PLAY

The amount of exercise your dog requires will vary greatly depending on his size, temperament and health. Keep in mind that it is not advisable to allow a dog to exercise much during the hottest part of the day. Rather, take him out for exercise in the mornings and evenings when it is cooler. An exercise routine should be discussed with your vet to ensure that it is properly geared to your dog's abilities.

Don't attempt to use exercise as a tool to tire a dog out or to completely control behavior problems. It may work for a short period of time, and exercise is always good for a healthy dog (as it is for a healthy person). But what an active dog really needs is a good balance of physical exercise and mental exercise. Working a dog's brain is a great way to tire him out and keep him sane. As with people, using your brain often uses up more energy than using your body.

There is obviously an enormous variety of ways to play with a dog. When playing with your dog, always keep in mind what effect it is having on your relationship. Is it enhancing the relationship or having a negative effect? Appropriate play should always enhance the relationship.

Many games that are acceptable for one dog may not be for another, because dogs' temperaments differ. Don't play any game that lets your dog get so overexcited that you don't feel you can get him back under control instantly. Test this by saying (and enforcing) a command such as Sit or Down. Be cautious about playing games that encourage your dog to use parts of you, or your personal possessions or clothes, as chew toys.

SLEEPING

Where your adult dog sleeps is a decision only you can make. Some people wouldn't dream of letting a dog on their bed, while others can't fall asleep without Fido curled up by their feet.

If your dog is not thoroughly house trained, or if you are having other control problems, it is not advisable to allow him to sleep with you until those problems have been resolved. If you choose to allow your dog to sleep with you, it is crucial that you maintain as much control in bed as anywhere else. This means that when you tell your dog to get off the bed he must do so right away. Any indication that he is challenging you, such as grumbling or growling, should be dealt with immediately. You should keep a leash on the dog at all times until the problem is resolved and use the leash to correct the dog if he does not get off the bed. It is not advisable to allow young puppies to sleep on your bed for the simple fact that they will inevitably have a house-breaking accident.

For young puppies who are still sleeping in their crate, it is a good idea to move the crate to different spots in the house at least every few days. It is much easier for you and the dog if he is comfortable sleeping in many different areas. I had one client whose dog was perfectly behaved in her crate. When the client and her husband decided to remodel their bedroom, they had to stay in the guest room for a few weeks. Their perfectly crate-trained dog turned into a wailing mess because she had never slept anywhere but in "her spot."

SPAYING AND NEUTERING

This is a subject you should discuss with your veterinarian. He or she will most likely recommend doing the procedure at around six months old, depending on how quickly your dog is sexually maturing. Neutering has the same effect of decreasing sexual activity at any age, but for the pet dog it is usually preferable that it be sooner rather than later so that inappropriate dominance and sexual behaviors do not become habits that neutering cannot affect.

Neutering is the responsible thing to do when faced with the huge problem of pet overpopulation. Accidents do happen, even if you don't plan on giving your dog the opportunity to wander.

Neutering also has very definite health benefits. Spaying a female before her first heat season has been proven to decrease her chances of developing breast, uterine and ovarian cancer. It will also completely eliminate any chance that she'll develop pyometra, a potentially lethal uterine infection.

Neutering your male dog will reduce his chances of developing prostate cancer and will eliminate the risk of testicular tumors. Having the procedure done at a young age will also make him less likely to engage in skirmishes with other dogs and less likely to mark his territory with urine.

If you have a male dog who exhibits a high level of aggression, neutering will decrease his natural aggressive drive, but it will not affect the aggressive habits your dog has adopted. Only training can do that.

KEEPING YOUR DOG IN THE YARD

Keeping your dog in a fenced yard is generally not a good idea. Your dog may be teased by passersby. They may toss objects in at the dog, he may bark and annoy the neighbors or, worst of all, he may escape or be stolen. Most dogs can get out of most yards if given enough incentive to do so—such as boredom, a passing animal or person or searching out a sexual mate. Instead, try to keep him inside and let him spend time in the yard when someone can supervise him.

If you really want him to spend more time outside, try a secured outdoor kennel that you can lock. If you choose to keep your dog outside for part of the day, make sure he always has clean, fresh water and adequate shade from the sun or sufficient heat, depending on the climate.

Never, never leave your dog outside all day. There is no such thing as an "outside dog."

Be sure your dog is properly identified at all times, indoors and out, in case he gets loose. You have many options in this regard. You can use a traditional tag attached to his collar, or you can have your dog tattooed or microchipped. You should talk to your vet about these options.

WHAT CAN YOU DO WITH A TRAINED DOG?

When you have a dog who knows how to behave in the human world, he is a pleasure to be around. It's only natural that you'll want to include him in more and more of your activities.

There are more dog-related activities across the country than you could do in a lifetime. Obedience and breed competitions have always been abundant, but recently sports, such as canine agility, flyball, terrier trials, field trials for hunting dogs and Frisbee competitions, have become very popular. Contact the American Kennel Club or a local dog club to find out more about these activities.

You can also get your dog certified by the American Kennel Club as a Canine Good Citizen and make visits with your well-behaved dog to local nursing homes, hospitals or schools. Contact these institutions to find out about their programs.

There are many other ways well-trained dogs serve their humans. Most people are familiar with guide dogs who are trained to assist the blind. Yet the idea of dogs trained to assist people who are physically impaired in other ways is still rather new. In fact, dogs are trained to assist people who are hearing impaired by alerting them to noises, such as phones ringing and alarms. They are also trained to aid people who are confined to wheelchairs, and some dogs have even been trained to alert their owners moments before they have an epileptic seizure so they have time to prepare and prevent injuries.

Fabian has trained numerous dogs to serve their owners in extraordinary ways. One of these dogs is Jada, a Rottweiler whose owner, Michelle, is confined to a wheelchair. Michelle had little control over Jada when she brought her to Fabian as a two-year-old. Now she is trained to retrieve objects for Michelle and to assist in many other ways. She has become an asset to Michelle, but more important, she is a friend. The bond between Jada and Michelle is obvious to anyone who meets them.

In June of 1995, Fabian formed the Women's Best Friend Club, an organization whose goal is to aid women who feel the need for support due to physical disabilities or a history of being a victim of physical violence. One of the services provided by this group is to train service and self-defense dogs for women.

The general public has often viewed dogs trained for self-defense as dangerous and unreliable. But the

Jada sits proudly by Michelle's side.

Eko is calm and accepting of someone approaching and hugging Lauren. Notice that he is so under control that Lauren is not even holding the leash.

Even when Billy approaches Lauren with a weapon, Eko is still calm and under Lauren's complete control.

Only when Lauren is in true physical danger will she ask Eko to defend her, as a last resort. When Lauren tells him to, Eko will instantly come back to her side.

majority of dogs trained for protection work are trained inappropriately and then placed in the wrong hands.

Furthermore, most dogs used for these purposes are not adequately evaluated to determine whether they have a suitably stable temperament. It is a misconception to believe that a dog who defends his owner must be highly aggressive. In reality, a good self-defense dog should have a calm, even temperament and truly like people.

Even a dog who has been trained to defend his owner in dire circumstances must be a civilized canine member of society. Any dog trained to defend someone must first have a completely solid understanding of the basic commands, and the owner must have complete control of her dog. Furthermore, only people who have a true need for a self-defense dog should even consider owning one. It is an enormous responsibility and requires much commitment and maintenance on the part of the owner.

Lauren is physically disabled due to a car accident in 1991. By the time she was 21, Lauren had undergone four operations that left her with metal rods in her spine. Approximately one year later she was physically assaulted by a man. At this point her self-esteem and confidence were almost completely lost.

Lauren's mother gave her one of her home-bred German Shepherds, Eko. Lauren took Eko to Fabian to be trained as a service dog and for self-defense. She is a founding member of the Women's Best Friend Club.

Striker shows off her exceptional athletic ability.

Striker jumps rope with the help of Fabian and Sharlene.

TRICKS AND TRAINING

The average pet dog needs to know only four basic commands in order to become a successful member of society. Tricks are an added bonus that can facilitate a deeper bond of communication and trust between dog and owner. Fabian has trained more than 100 dogs to perform advanced tricks. Most of these dogs are trained for television commercials, but quite often the dogs perform their skills at training seminars and demonstrations. This is not to exploit the dogs, but to help people see what dogs can do. Once their interest is piqued, people are more receptive to understanding the dogs' capacity for learning and to accepting dogs in their communities and their lives.

Fabian's number one trick dog is Striker. She is a three-year-old Belgian Malinois who had three previous owners and a history of aggression toward

Striker carefully maneuvers a 10-foot-high tightrope. Every trick is carefully planned and monitored to ensure the dog's safety.

people. She had been bred to be used primarily as a protection dog and had gone through numerous trainers' hands. All of them passed her on saying she was "too crazy."

Striker was scheduled to be euthanized when Fabian rescued her. After two months of love and training they were both guests on *Late Night With David Letterman.*

It was no miracle that turned Striker around. And Fabian does not even feel that Striker is any more intelligent than most of the other dogs he works with. Her ability to learn the behaviors he has taught her is due more to her drive and athletic ability.

Fabian simply spent the time teaching Striker which behaviors were acceptable and which were not. He was very fair with her and careful to not become emotional if he felt frustrated or upset. When he did focus on her, it was to lavishly praise and encourage her.

Once Striker learned what the boundaries were, Fabian had established a strong foundation of trust. The foundation is so strong that Striker seems willing to do just about anything Fabian asks, because she is so sure that he is her guide and will watch out for her. This should be the goal of every pet dog owner.

Lena, a Doberman Pinscher, jumps gracefully through Andrea's arms.

WRITE TO FABIAN AT:

BACK TO BASICS

518 ROUTE 211 W

MIDDLETOWN, NY

10940

INDEX